The Definitive Guide for Novice to Expert

Defensive Handgun Skills

by David Fessenden

Published by

Gun Digest® Books, an imprint of F+W Media, Inc.
Krause Publications • 700 East State Street • Iola, WI 54990-0001
715-445-2214 • 888-457-2873
www.krausebooks.com

To order books or other products call toll-free 1-800-258-0929
or visit us online at www.krausebooks.com, www.gundigeststore.com
or www.Shop.Collect.com

Library of Congress Control Number: 2010924665

ISBN-13: 978-1-4402-1381-6
ISBN-10: 1-4402-1381-X

Cover Design by Tom Nelsen
Designed by Paul Birling
Edited by Dan Shideler
Cover photo courtesy of Wiley X Eyewear

Printed in United States of America

The author wishes to extend his heartfelt and warm thanks to all those who offered encouragement and assistance in the writing of this book:

First, my sister, Nancy B. Fessenden, PhD., who completed the first proofreading of several of my early chapters. Her critique and comments were directly responsible for the direction of this book.

I would like to thank my friend and fellow author Eric Lawrence for his comments and assistance in the composition of the book. Eric also proofread all the chapters. Congratulations, Eric, on the continued success of your two new books.

Many thanks to my lady friends, colleagues and authors Alean (Ali) Pray and Kathleen Kingston for spending many long evening hours doing the final proofreading on this effort. I owe you both much, good friends.

In the photography department, I wish to thank Jason Winder of Winder Works.com in Parker, Colorado for his time, talent and expertise in taking dozens of pictures for the book. Getting these pictures perfect was quite a chore. Well done, Jason.

Also in the regard to the photography in the book, many many thanks to both of my models, Dave from Aurora, Colorado, and Rhisa Dawn Oler of Castle Rock, Colorado. They both donated several days of photo shoots for our "How-To" section. They showed considerable professionalism and patience in the face of weather that wasn't always that cooperative. Thank you many times over, Dave and Rhisa.

I would also like to give a huge thank you to Brandon Baker, the owner of Rocky Mountain Guns and Ammo in Parker, Colorado, for his counsel, help and donation of items that appear in the photograph in the Weapons and Gear chapter of the book. Many thanks again, Brandon.

Lastly, I wish to give a huge thank you to Dan Shideler and all the folks at Gun Digest Books for their faith in this heretofore-unpublished author.

Finally, to anyone else I may have inadvertently forgotten, many thanks to you, too!

David L. Fessenden
Elizabeth, Colorado

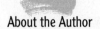

David Fessenden is a gun collector and a firearms instructor and restorer. David started his teaching career after obtaining an NRA certification for pistol, rifle and shotgun and taught CCW and personal protection classes in Colorado in the 1990s. While working as an armed security officer for a Denver-based retail food corporation in late 1999, he was invited to Front Sight FTI in Pahrump, Nevada, to attend an Instructor Development course. Upon completing the course, he was asked to join Front Sight's staff. After five years as a firearms instructor, he retired and moved back to Colorado. He now lives in Elizabeth, Colorado, and teaches his growing defensive handgun classes in Wiggins and Aurora, Colorado, on a regular basis.

"Self-defence is Nature's eldest law."

John Dryden (1631-1700), English poet, dramatist, critic.
Absalom and Achitophel.

Defensive Handgun Skills

Table of Contents

Preface

As a young boy, I grew up in a small town just northwest of Boston, Massachusetts, in a non-gun owning family. I was exposed to an occasional .22 rifle or a 12-gauge shotgun on summer family trips to New Hampshire or Maine.

My cousin in Portland had a new semiautomatic .22 rifle with a scope on it and we would occasionally venture off to the town dump to shoot rats. Of course, this was a rare and new experience for me and one that I looked forward to during every visit. At this point in my life, I didn't consciously feel that firearms would ever become a major interest in my adult life.

In high school, similar opportunities to shoot popped up now and again and I always jumped at the chance to shoot with my friends. I thoroughly enjoyed these outings. While in the U.S. Marine Corps in the early 1950's, I was trained on just about every weapons system "the Corps" had, but I viewed this as more of a military obligation than a form of personal pleasure. I shot Expert with the M-1 Garand and carried a Colt 1911A1 .45 ACP pistol for over a year while stationed overseas. I was finally able to shoot Sharpshooter with the 1911A1.

I began, through these experiences, to realize that I had a talent for firearms, but I was focused on going back to college and completing my education. In college, I went hunting once with a fraternity brother but found I didn't enjoy it and have never hunted since. I bought a Lee Enfield .303 British SMLE bolt-action rifle from this same fraternity brother, sporterized it and took a girlfriend out into the hills for a recreational shoot. If memory serves me correctly, she wasn't too impressed and that ended any further shooting with her. She was obviously into other forms of outdoor activities.

While raising a family and climbing the corporate ladder, my shooting opportunities were few and far between and it wasn't until that obligatory midlife divorce and a move to California that I discovered firearms for good. The group of friends that I socialized with all enjoyed shooting and soon we spent our weekends at the "River" on the California/Arizona border. Shooting became a very important part of our daily routine there. I purchased a Browning M1935 Hi-Power 9mm pistol and began to learn everything I could about it. I trained myself in its use by viewing videos and reading all the books I could get my hands on. Seeking professional training had not become important to me yet. I then began buying more pistols and collecting guns, by acquiring old Winchester lever guns, M-1 carbines and Garands.

A little over 10 years ago, I took an NRA Firearms Instructors Class and became a certified instructor in Pistol, Rifle and Shotgun. In 1999, I attended and passed an Instructors Development Course at Front Sight F.T.I. in Pahrump, Nevada, and was immediately invited to join their staff of instructors. Initially, I worked on the submachine range. I was later assigned to pistol, rifle and shotgun ranges for over the nearly five years I was there. I spent the vast majority of my time teaching the Defensive Handgun courses, both two- and four-day versions. In that time, we trained around 10,000 students.

I worked with some exceptionally talented instructors and met hundreds of equally fine and enthusiastic students. I also got to teach many celebrities and prominent law enforcement officers. It was the experience and chance of a lifetime to accomplish something that I felt I was, and still am, very good at and at that moment wanted very much to do. I was able to develop a true synergy with all my students and was always able to raise the level of performance in each and every student I came in contact with. This served to galvanize my passion for teaching and with it my vision of perfecting what I refer to as the Art of Defensive Guncraft courses, and hence this book.

David Fessenden
Aurora, Colorado
Spring, 2010

"The Second Amendment states that 'the right of the people to keep and bear arms shall not be infringed,' period. There is no mention of magazine size, rate of fire or to what extent these arms resemble assault rifles. All rifles were assault rifles in those days. Futhermore, if the gun laws that Massachusetts has now, had been in force in 1776, we'd all be Canadians, and you know what kind of weather Canada has."

P.J. O'Rourke, U.S. Journalist, "Parliament of Whores", 1991

Throughout this handbook, you should be aware that I am consciously keeping all of my points, statements and assertions as simple as I can. I do not wish to burden you with mounds and piles of excruciating detail, data and boring minutiae. Many authors, in an effort to fill pages, will drone on ad nauseam on a subject at hand and then, to compound the problem, start repeating themselves on the subject. This would put you to sleep, I'm sure.

I will keep this book interesting and simple. I have written it for the law-abiding gun owner who may not possess an extensive background in firearms or firearms training or who may just be starting out on his journey toward the mastery of firearms gun handling and marksmanship excellence. Therefore, for those folks, I again pledge to make my book as readable, understandable and interesting for all my readers to enjoy. The premise of this treatise is to therefore set the table for the text that will follow, as I begin my presentation on defensive handgun skills.

I have laid out the experiences and qualifications that I feel lend credence to my abilities to undertake this challenge. In writing this book, I am reaching out to the responsible armed citizen and sharing my experiences and expertise with the reader, one armed citizen to another. Many current books are written by retired law enforcement officers, gun writers and military personnel. There is certainly nothing wrong with this and I really have no heartburn with it, but my point is that their experiences and backgrounds inevitably are reflected in their writings. They end up espousing the techniques and experiences that they are most familiar with and their books end up teaching civilians from that perspective. I feel my book is unique in that it teaches defensive gun handling and marksmanship techniques to armed citizens from another armed citizen.

We will look at every aspect of defensive guncraft – the people and forces that have shaped and molded it and that continue to influence and define its present development. The history and philosophy of how defensive gun craft evolved will be looked at, in some detail, along with the legal ramifications of concealed carry and the necessary gear to safely carry out this awesome responsibility. The proper combat mindset needed to center your training and raise your level of proficiency and awareness is covered in sufficient detail to guide you on this most important of journeys.

Be careful, be safe, and be armed.

Chapter 1

The Definition of Defensive Handgun Skills

Before we can explore the realm of defensive handgun skills, we need to agree on a definition of what this art form truly is. Bear in mind that we must work within the confines of the legal constraints imposed by many state legislatures.

Most of the 38-odd states that have passed shall-issue concealed carry laws all have varying clauses in each statute. One common thread in each is that you have the right to protect your life and that of your family, and your property, from the threat of serious bodily harm and/or death. Pretty basic stuff, that! Therein lies the essence of our definition: you do not have to be a victim.

The essence of defensive handgun skills is simply this: you do not have to be a victim!

My rationale for defensive guncraft goes as follows: you have the right to use a weapon (handgun, long gun or edged weapon) in the lawful protection of your life and that of your family. It may be used as a deterrent or as lethal force, if the assailant launches a lethal and violent attack.

It follows, then, that the definition of defensive handgun skills is simply this: they are the means of using a weapon (hand gun, long gun or edged weapon) in the lawful protection of your life and that of your family. Now this definition has not been pulled from some other publication or author's work. It is mine and comes from my study, research, teaching and thoughts about the various state laws and their application to our Constitution.

> *The definition of defensive handgun skills is simply this: they are the means of using a weapon (hand gun, long gun or edged weapon) in the lawful protection of your life and that of your family.*

One note, at this point: several anti-gun states still cling to the silly notion that the potential victim must demonstrate to an attacker that he has retreated to a position of being less of a threat to said attacker. Now this doesn't make a lot of sense. Currently, several states have stricken this clause from their statutes in favor of the potential victim, in the form of what is now being called Stand Your Ground laws. Finally, some of these state legislatures at least get it! Remember that you and you alone are responsible for knowing all applicable laws dealing with personal protection in the state in which you reside.

We know that law enforcement cannot always be there in our time of greatest peril, so we must train to prepare ourselves for this eventuality, should it ever occur. We have to train so as to confine our responses within the legal limits imposed by each individual statute. You see, concealed carry weapon (CCW) laws are all double edged. They provide the law-abiding citizen with the legal tools needed to provide for his or her own protection, but they demand that he or she act with great restraint and stay within this narrow band of responsibility in regard to a criminal who is intent on doing bodily harm. If the CCW permit holder operates within these limits of force, identifies each level of danger and escalation by his assailant, and applies the appropriate measured response and survives the encounter, then he or she may still have to face the legal system in his or her community in a civil action, as deemed necessary under the law, by the district attorney.

The CCW permit comes with a tremendous and awesome responsibility to react to a threat with a controlled response that is sufficiently measured but also forceful enough to stop the threat. Remember, it is not a license to shoot a bad guy who may only appear to mean you great harm. Identifying that level of the threat is a very important component of your training.

Please note that my definition of defensive guncraft has been carefully formulated to remain within the bounds of most legal terminology and to comply in a generic way with basic CCW statutes.

One last time on our definition of the art of defensive handgun skills: they are the means of using a weapon (hand gun, long gun or edged weapon) in the lawful protection of your life and that of your family. They can be deployed as a deterrent or as lethal force, if the assailant continues a potentially lethal and violent attack.

Now, let's examine all the elements of our defensive handgun skills equation and construct a logical sequence that will afford us a better understanding of this lifesaving and often necessary art.

Familiarity and proficiency with your chosen weapon are only half the requirement. You must also be aware of, and observe, all applicable laws governing concealed carry in your state.

U.S. Naval Academy, Annapolis, Maryland. Instruction in pistol shooting - 1942

Chapter 2

The History of Defensive Guncraft

As most of us know, there have been primitive firearms around since the mid-1300s. Of course, over the centuries, they evolved into the sophisticated weapons systems that we can see on the battlefields and in the hunting, recreational and sporting venues spread around the world. So how did the theory and principles of defensive hand gunning emerge? Good question.

For the answer, we need to look back to World War II and to Lt. Col. Jeff Cooper and the evolution of his fast draw and combat shoots that were staged at Big Bear Lake, California, in the 1950s. Up until that time, handgun shooting consisted of one-handed target shooting with none of the run-and-gun tactics that we see employed today at many of the IPSC and IDPA venues. This concept would change considerably under the guidance of Col. Cooper and his Big Bear contests in the next decade.

In fact, I was serving in the Marine Corps during this time and learned to shoot my 1911A1 duty pistol in this old time Camp Perry-style, one-handed technique with the firing side arm horizontal, locked out, and my body perpendicular to the target. It was often referred to as the dueling position. Cooper's Big Bear shoots, by their very nature, were spawning grounds for experimentation and innovation as each competitor worked to get a competitive edge over his fellow competitors.

Initially, they used revolvers as their weapon of choice. Cooper started shooting his 1911A1 Colt Commander, which he had trained with while an officer in the Marine Corps. As his tournament wins grew in number, more and more of his fellow competitors took note and switched to various semiautomatics, mainly 1911-type weapons. Even Thell Reed, the King of the Single Actions, eventually switched to the 1911A1. All experimented with movement and combat (tactical) applications with this handgun.

Developed by the late Jack Weaver, the Weaver Stance is the classic defensive handgunning posture.

One such innovator was L.A. County Sheriff's Deputy Jack Weaver. He worked on several stances and grips over time and figured out that a more stable and aggressive two-handed grip would afford him the accuracy, speed and precision he needed. At first he aimed his weapon at the target in a semi-point-shoot method. To improve his consistency and precision during the shoots, Weaver experimented with raising the weapon higher to eye level for precision-aimed shots. His accuracy and winning percentages improved immediately. Thus was born the Weaver Stance and Grip. (I discuss the Weaver Stance and Grip in great detail later in this book.) It consists of a 30° bladed stance with the firing-side foot pulled back about four to six inches from the firing line and combined with an overlapping two-handed grip.

> *"Well, in the first place, an*
> *armed society is a polite society."*
>
> A partial quote from a Robert Heinlein book, spoken to Mordan Claude
> "Beyond the Horizon". 1942

The Weaver Stance and Grip proved to be a winner. It assisted in managing recoil and allowed Weaver to deliver rapid-fire multiple shots with considerable accuracy. Soon, his fellow shooters adopted this shooting position and today the Weaver is universally used by all shooters in the field of defensive guncraft. (Jack Weaver passed away in Carson City, Nevada, in July of 2009.)

Cooper's shooting tournaments were initially called Leather Slaps and were essentially blank-firing fast-draw contests. They became very popular with the viewing public, but soon evolved into true combat-style action shoots, combining movement with time limitations. Cooper held them exclusively at the newly-opened ski resort atop Tejon Pass, in San Bernardino county, California. He called his group the Bear Valley Gunslingers. (This ski resort is still there today and is now called Snow Summit.)

As the popularity of Cooper's contests spread, the two-handed Weaver stance and grip were being emulated by the shooting public all over the southwest. The name of Cooper's organization had now become the South West Combat Pistol League. New shooting clubs formed teams to participate in this new and exciting form of pistol competition.

It is at this point that Cooper began to form the nucleus of what was to become his Modern Technique of the Pistol. It contained the basic elements of his form of modern pistol shooting and its combat nature, compared to the older Camp Perry style of static competitive and recreational shooting of the past.

Training under the guidance of a qualified, certified instructor is the best way to build defensive handgun skills.

The Big Bear shoots gave impetus and seed to combat shooting for the public at large and many big-name shooters rushed to join Cooper and compete in them: Bob Munden, Ray Chapman, Eldon Carl, Thell Reed, John Shaw, Mickey Fowler, Mike Dalton and Armend Swenson, to name just a few.

As the popularity of this sport grew, spurred on by the many TV westerns, some of the fledging anti-gun groups of the day petitioned the California Secretary of State's office to change the name of the SWCPL. They objected to the use of the word "combat" in the name. The California legislature caved in to the offended group and informed Cooper that the name had to be changed. Cooper acquiesced and renamed his club the International Practical Shooters Confederation. Thus was born what we now refer to as IPSC!

With IPSC established and a bad taste in his mouth for California and its brand of politics, Cooper left the IPSC management group and took his combat shooting and movement tactics and moved to Arizona. There, Cooper started his American Pistol Institute (API), in Paulden, Arizona. He later changed the name to Gunsite Firearms Training Center. He devoted himself to training both civilians and law enforcement personnel in the techniques of personal protection that were formulated during his Big Bear shooting days. At Gunsite, he instituted his Modern Techniques of the Pistol into the curriculum of his defensive handgun classes. Now civilians and law enforcement students were being taught the techniques that proved so successful during the competition that Cooper and his pals conducted at Big Bear Lake. His classes covered all the principles of movement, aggressiveness, tactics, mindset, the Weaver stance, gun handling, marksmanship and pistol deployment, coupled with his thoughts on speed, precision and accuracy. This, folks, is the precursor to what we now call defensive guncraft and its correlation to personal protection with a handgun. We have Col. Cooper and his sharp mind and wit to thank for his contribution to our welfare.

Gunsite is today rated as one of the top firearms training facilities in the country, along with Front Sight, Thunder Ranch and LFI. Cooper spent his remaining years writing, lecturing, consulting and operating and teaching at Gunsite. Through a couple of ownership changes, Cooper stayed at Gunsite until his health began to fail and he finally passed away on the September 26, 2006, at his home, the Sconce, on the Gunsite property.

The passage of the first CCW law in the country in 1987, in Florida, gave further impetus to the need for professional training in the art of defensive handgun skills. History has borne this out – in recent years a veritable boom in gun ownership has occurred, along with the growth of firearms training facilities. Not coincidentally, numerous peer-researched surveys all show an overall reduction in violent gun-related crime across our country. All this has served to enhance the reputation of Col. Jeff Cooper as the genius who was responsible for the development of the principles of defensive handgun skills.

"If all Americans want is security, they can go to prison. They'll have enough to eat, a bed and a roof over their heads, but if an American wants to preserve his dignity and his equality as a human being, he must not bow his neck to any government."

Dwight David Eisenhower, speech in Galveston, Texas. December 8, 1949.
New York Times. Dec.9, 1949 p.23.

Chapter 3

Gun Safety

No book on firearms training that deals with gun handling and marksmanship would be complete without a thorough, up-front discussion of gun safety.

Safety, more especially gun safety, is a major concern for those shooters on and around any gun range when firearms are present. A professional, focused demeanor must be exhibited by all shooters at all times. Any reckless, careless, unsafe and unprofessional gun handling or behavior will never be tolerated or condoned by any observers or fellow shooters. This type of behavior will only demonstrate to all of those in your presence your level of incompetence and your total disrespect for their general safety and welfare. Contrary to this disrespect and reckless disregard for safety, a focused and concerned gun owner must always exhibit proper and correct safety standards whether on the range or alone in the field engaged in recreational shooting.

Remember, always handle your firearms in a safe and responsible manner and keep your head in the game! Further, the Four Universal Rules of Firearms Safety are in effect 24/7 wherever and whenever a firearm is present. Let's start by discussing the importance of the Four Universal Rules of Firearms Safety.

The Four Universal Rules of Firearms Safety

These rules are attributed to Col. Cooper before he became a major influence in the handgun training field; there were, and still are, those who espoused dozens of such rules. Most of these rules were simply reiterations of the others. Recently I saw a modem firearms training video in which the instructor proposed that there were 16 rules of firearms safety. The vast majority of them were silly and insulted the viewer's intelligence. Anyone with a half a room-temperature IQ could have routinely figured out that breaking a couple of them, while on the range, would not put them in any great peril. Cooper culled out all these nonsensical rules and relegated them to the trash heap. Breaking any one of the remaning rules while shooting or training with your firearm, however, might result in death or injury to the shooter and/or his fellow range companions.

Col. Cooper subsequently modified and distilled this hodgepodge of useless and repetitive rules into his Four Universal Rules of Firearms Safety. Any instructor worth his reputation should faithfully promote them on his range or in his classes. I teach them with much passion and ask my students to recite them verbatim in front of their fellow students each day until they are all able to exhibit that they have them firmly committed to memory.

Stephan P. Wenger, in his book Defensive Use of Firearms, has added a fifth rule, which states "maintain control of your gun." My feeling is that this line of reasoning is more pertinent to gun ownership and storage than to range safety. It relates to the legal problems that can accrue from having your firearm fall into the wrong hands and end up being used in the commission of a felony offense like armed robbery, murder or the wrongful death of a minor. In many states, you can be charged as an accessory to that crime, the thought being that through your negligence, you facilitated the commission of the crime. Wenger's fifth rule makes a lot of sense and all gun owners should be mindful of its implications. However, I choose not to include it as part of the original four rules. It goes without saying that proper and lawful gun storage of firearms by all gun owners is of the utmost importance at all times.

Rule #1 Treat all weapons as if they are loaded.

Many gun pundits reverse these sentiments when reciting the Four Universal Rules of Firearms Safety and say "All weapons are always loaded!" To me, there is a very obvious distinction here and it may be parsing words, but all weapons are not always loaded. A popular talk show host has a saying that I

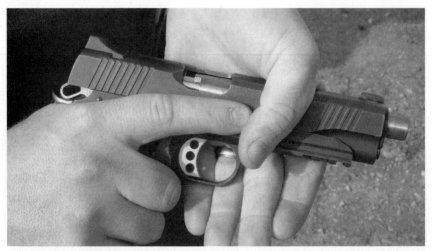

Is this weapon loaded or unloaded? It's impossible to tell without checking the chamber. Thus the rule: Treat all weapons as if they are loaded!

utilize in my class lectures and writings: Words have meaning and actions have consequences! Think about that for a while, please.

When you are cleaning your weapon and have chamber-checked it several times and it is now field-stripped and lying on your bench, is it loaded? Of course not. When you have decided that you need to send your weapon off to a gunsmith for a certain repair job and you have chamber checked it several times, removed the magazine and partially disassembled it, is it loaded? No. My point is that a broad-brush statement such as "all weapons are always loaded" simply does not ring true 100% of the time. For example, is a gun in a holster always loaded? True, we must always treat them as if they are loaded, and before putting them into our holsters or placing them in a gun safe or handing them to a fellow student, we need to conduct a chamber check or two. Remember, chamber checking is two seconds of cheap insurance!

Rule #2. Do not point the muzzle at anything you are not willing to destroy.

This is quintessential Cooper and refers to muzzle awareness. The muzzle of your gun is the opening at the end of the barrel out of which the bullet exits when the weapon is fired. Waving your weapon around irresponsibly on the range or in a crowd of fellow shooters on the range is highly unsafe and very disrespectful toward the safety of those around you. You could be covering them with the muzzle. By covering them, I am referring to the physical act of tracking or crossing your friend's body parts with the muzzle of the gun. It does not have to come in physical contact with them.

Keep that muzzle clear of all body parts – including your own!

Who is the biggest culprit when it comes to muzzling someone? You are. In many of your gun handling drills, you will accidentally cover yourself dozens of times. While re-holstering, a new student sometimes places his support-side hand on his holster, to steady it and draw the weapon across his exposed hand. If this were a loaded firearm and you suddenly became muzzle-aware, you would immediately feel the need to never place your hand there again. The safest place for your muzzle to be pointed is always downrange while performing any of the gun handling drills. If that is not an option, then point it toward the ground, finger off the trigger. It should never be pointed anywhere near a fellow student or instructor.

Speaking as an instructor who has had dozens of guns pointed at him on the range, I get very grumpy whenever it occurs! In my defensive handgun classes, we demonstrate how this can happen (with our "index finger gun") and how to become hyper-muzzle conscious.

Rule #3. Keep your finger off of the trigger and out of the trigger guard until you are pointing it at your intended target.

I consider the trigger guard to be part of the trigger itself. Resting your trigger finger across the trigger guard is a practice that is fraught with potential disaster. If something startles you and you flinch or pull back while in this condition, your trigger finger will pull right back on the trigger and fire off an ND (negligent discharge).

Safe position for trigger finger during practice drills: on the frame and NOT on the trigger guard!

Therefore, get in the habit of placing your trigger finger on the frame of your weapon while you are engaged in any gun handling drills or at the ready position. The only time you may place your trigger finger on the trigger is when you are pointing it at your intended target.

When not pointed at the target or resting at the ready position, your trigger finger must stay firmly pressed against the frame of your weapon, well above the trigger guard. Where, exactly? It depends on the handgun and the length of your trigger finger. Every handgun has a home base or tactile reference point. It can be an exposed shaft end or screw head that the shooter can feel with his trigger finger. The tip of your trigger finger must reside there, unless your gun is pointed at the target and you have made a conscious decision to fire it. With a revolver, your trigger finger should reside right under the cylinder, exactly as described above.

Rule #4. Know what is between you and your intended target and what is beyond.

When you're shooting under the control of a range master, this rule may pale a bit in importance, simply because he has checked the range and deemed it safe to commence the range work at hand. He has done all the work for you. His commands to you state that the range is clear and it is safe to commence with the firing exercise. Nobody is between you and your target or behind said target.

A safe shooting environment: nothing between the shooter and the target and a well-defined, impenetrable backstop.

Out on the street, however, it is a totally different set of circumstances. You must make the determination that it is safe for you to present your weapon and possibly fire at your adversary. If you make the decision to exercise your constitutionally-guaranteed right to self-protection and fire two shots at your assailant and they either miss or overpenetrate and continue down range, the chance is great that one or both of these bullets could strike an innocent bystander. Now you have a Rule #4 violation, possibly a tragic one.

If you had practiced what we call situational awareness and looked beyond your suspected assailant and seen, for example, that a child was playing in her front yard before you presented your weapon, you might have decided that the shot was not safe and had adopted another strategy. If the worst had happened and a bystander were injured, you would now probably have a major legal battle on your hands, either criminal or civil – hence the expression that the only good gunfight is the one that you are able to avoid.

The Four Universal Rules of Firearms Safety

Rule #1 Treat all weapons as if they are loaded.

Rule #2. Do not point the muzzle at anything you are not willing to destroy.

Rule #3. Keep your finger off of the trigger and out of the trigger guard until you are pointing it at your intended target.

Rule #4. Know what is between you and your intended target and what is beyond.

Chamber Checking

Chamber checking is often described as "two seconds of cheap insurance." It is just that. Chamber checking is the inspection of the chamber of any weapon to determine the status or condition of the chamber or chambers, i.e., is the weapon empty or is it loaded? Unless stipulated in the description, all techniques are for a right-handed shooter.

Semiautomatics

Chamber Checking the Semi-Automatic: "Hand Under Dust Cover" Method

Hand under the dust cover. First thumb back the hammer with your support-side thumb. Bring your support-side hand down under the dust cover of the weapon and place your support-side thumb on the left side of the slide with your index and middle finger gripping the right side of the slide.

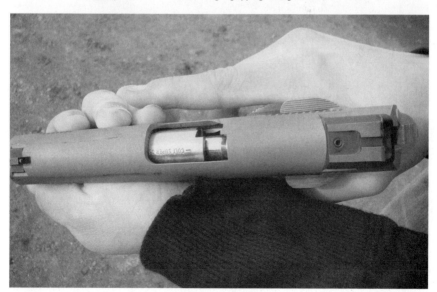

Press back to the rear with your support-side hand and crack the ejection port open about ¼". Look inside the chamber area for the presence of or the lack of brass. Release the slide to go home under its own spring tension.

Chamber Checking the Semi-Automatic: "Wedge" Method *continued*

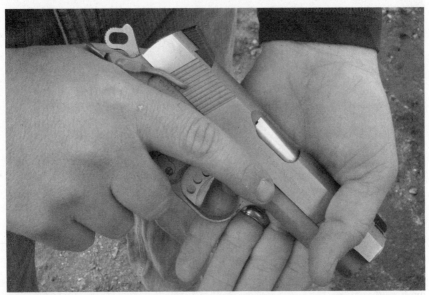

Thumb back the hammer with your support-side thumb. Holding the weapon in your firing-side hand, place the web of your support-side hand against the front and top of the slide. Grip the vertical sides of the slide with your index finger and thumb. Grip very tight with both.

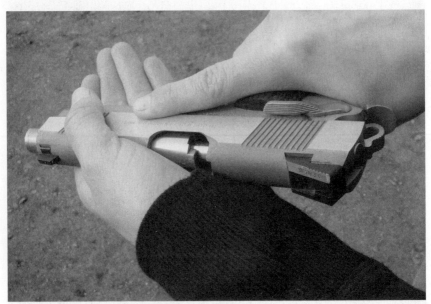

The top of the slide should be held securely in that grip. Close down with all the fingers of your support-side hand and press to the rear. Crack the ejection port open about ¼" and inspect for brass or the lack thereof. This gun has a cartridge in the chamber. Release the slide to close shut under its own spring tension.

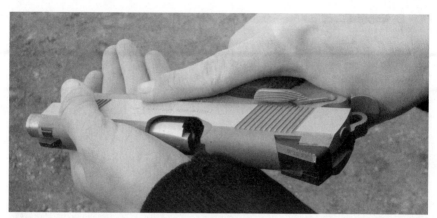

This gun does not have a cartridge in the chamber. Release the slide to close shut under its own spring tension.

Chamber Checking the Semi-Automatic: "Claw" Method

Another method, "The Claw," is is sometimes used on semiautos that do not have exposed hammers but do have slide-mounted decocking levers and no exposed hammer.

To chamber check using the Claw Method:

Hold the weapon in your support-side hand.

Place your firing-side thumb on the tang of the weapon while engaging both ears of the decocking lever on the slide with your index and middle finger of the firing-side hand.

Chamber Checking the Semi-Automatic: "Claw" Method *continued*

Now press the slide to the rear by squeezing your fingers to the rear, using your thumb as a fulcrum, thus cracking the ejection open ¼". Check for the presence or lack thereof of brass in the chamber area. Release the slide.

Revolvers

Chamber Checking the Revolver

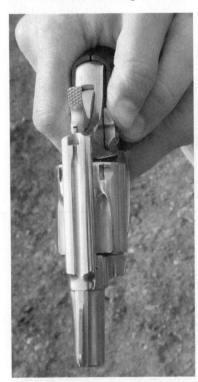 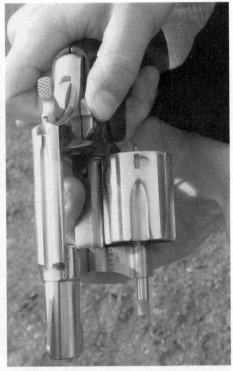

Holding the weapon in your firing side hand, press the cylinder latch (release) forward or pull it backward, depending on the make or model.

With the index and middle finger of your support-side hand, press the cylinder out of the centerline of the weapon, to the left.

Look into and inspect each chamber for the presence of spent or live cartridges. This cylinder is fully loaded.

To close the cylinder, press it backward to the left into the centerline of the weapon with your support-side thumb.

Chamber-checking is an excellent habit to build. Get into it!

PRACTICAL PISTOL SHOOTING

the state of the art in 1970

A two-fisted shooting technique that develops skilled, combat-effective handgunners. Yet it's been long derided and condemned by the Establishment—military, police and civilian—with little or no justification.

by JEFF COOPER

The author demonstrates the standard Weaver hold, suitable for some 80% of combat pistol problems.

IN OUR AMAZEMENT at the scientific marvels of the modern age we sometimes overlook the fact that improvement in human capacity has almost paralleled the development of the machine. Particularly since WW II, the records of athletic achievement have been broken so frequently that we might wonder if our ancestors were really trying. Abstract barriers like the four-minute-mile have been shown to be illusory, and we are led to the conclusion that the potential of the human body, directed by the coordinating genius of the human mind, is practically limitless. In no field of endeavor is this more evident than in pistol shooting, where the events of the past 20 years have completely revolutionized the technique of the handgun, and have effectively altered the nature of the tool—in the hands of those who have followed and understood developments. Specifically, modern techniques have changed the pistol from an emergency, last-ditch, arm's length, in conclusive instrument into a very serious weapon, demonstrably superior, in trained hands, to many of the long arms that were thought to have superseded it. We are now able to pose simulated combat problems for the pistol which cannot be handled as well with rifle, shotgun, or submachine gun. This would not have been thought possible in 1940, yet it is accomplished with weapons designed near the turn of the century. It is a human, not a mechanical, achievement.

The reasons for this lie in the abandonment of two traditional concepts: first, the separation of marksmanship standards from efficient weaponcraft; and second, the organizational system of training.

The traditional definition of a good pistol shot has always been based upon the ability to perform an unrealistic task. Today, if one were to ask the president of the International Shooting Union to name the world's greatest shot he would name a man who almost certainly would stand no chance at all in what the pistol pioneers call a "serious" pistol contest. His ability to fire a two-inch group from offhand at 50 meters in 20 minutes with a 22 free pistol would be useful, but it would not be enough, because he would need the additional skill to dominate a major-caliber, fight-stopping instrument and he would need to dominate it quickly. As long as sidearm competition remains unrelated to the primary purpose of the sidearm, which is self-defense, mastery of such competition proves only that the champion can perform a difficult exercise in nerve control, not that he is adequately armed when carrying a pistol.

Similarly, if one were to ask a conventional NRA pistol shooter what con-

Col. Jeff Cooper, here shown in a Gun Digest article from 1971, developed many of the principles of defensive guncraft.

Chapter 4

Cooper's Enduring Principles

We have examined and established the history of and the definition of the art of defensive guncraft. Now, let's explore in more detail the principles or influences that help us to reinforce and fortify the tenets of this art. They bolster and energize our beliefs and guide us on our journey toward a mastery of the handgun. They will aid us in understanding and reaching our goal of attaining the mindset we call the Comfort of Skill at Arms. (I will discuss the Comfort of Skill at Arms in detail later.) Indeed, you must have a total mastery of these factors before you learn all the firearms skills necessary to competently and safely handle your firearm. View them as the foundation upon which you construct your skill level, layer by layer up this ladder of firearms proficiency. These principles are as follows:

- The Four Universal Rules of Firearms Safety
- The Color Code of Mental Awareness
- The Modem Technique of the Pistol
- Cooper's Principles of Personal Defense

We have already discussed the Four Universal Rules of Firearms Safety. Let's examine the remaining principles in detail, along with other experts' perspectives.

> *"When you disarm your subject you offend them by showing that either from cowardliness or lack of faith, you distract them; and either conclusion will induce them to hate."*
>
> Niccolo Machiavelli (1469-1527), the Prince1514.

The Color Codes of Mental Awareness

This is another gem from the mind of Jeff Cooper. Here, Cooper states that there are several levels of awareness that a person must be in at all times during the day. They are essential to giving oneself a chance to spot trouble that may be coming his or her way and may also allow time to survive the threat. Cooper did not create these principles but refined and compiled them from his days in the Marine Corps, adapting them for civilian use. The conditions are as follows:

#1. Condition White

This is the lowest form of awareness and consists of a total lack thereof. In this condition, you could be run over by a steamroller or about to be hit over the head with a baseball bat and not even see it coming.

#2. Condition Yellow

This is a condition of relaxed awareness and is the condition that all people must be in at all times. In condition yellow, you are observing and alert to all that is going on about you. You are making mental notes on all these activities. You will not betray to these folks that you are cognizant of their activities, so as to not telegraph to them your alert condition.

In Condition Yellow, for example, you might observe an individual wearing a heavy sweatshirt in 90° weather. He appears overdressed and definitely out of place compared to everyone else in the immediate area. This may trigger some level of concern in you. What is he hiding under that sweatshirt? Your Condition Yellow has served you well thus far.

#3. Condition Orange

To continue the example, you now realize or sense that the person in the sweatshirt is following you to your car and, from his body language, you can tell that he is up to no good. His hand is moving to his waistband. Sensing an imminent threat, you are in Condition Orange.

#4. Condition Red

You now see the threat and recognize the need to take immediate action to insure your safety. His hand is now on the handle of a knife or revolver frame that he is withdrawing from under that sweatshirt. You have confirmed the threat and are in Condition Red.

#5. Condition Black

In Condition Black, you take defensive action. Your training kicks in and you take steps to ensure that you are protected. You may flee the area or stand and defend yourself with anything from pepper spray to lethal force.

Follow me on this: I believe thoroughly in and teach the Color Code of Mental Awareness but find that the last two levels, Red and Black, are not really about awareness in the strictest sense. Rather they are levels of action, in that at that point in the process, you need to act somehow. Your survival mode training kicks in and you are no longer simply observant. In order to survive the threat, you must act in some manner.

Some may argue that I am splitting hairs here, but you must understand the complexity of the awareness picture and the point at which things become actionable as the scenario unfolds. A purely robotic approach to these important factors may result in someone dead or hurt. I am totally comfortable with teaching all five conditions as a legitimate part of Cooper's Code.

Above—At the Air Force Academy—Cooper illustrates the left-hand position from a barricade. • Right—The author demonstrates the two-hand kneeling stance with the 45 auto.

Cooper's early defensive guncraft courses were a far cry from many of today's high-tech seminars.

Lawrence's Three Elements of Awareness

Eric Lawrence, in his instructional shooter's book *The Operator's Tactical Pistol Shooting Manual*, offers these three tenents of awareness that can be important to whether a potential victim will survive a potentially violent attack:

1. Perceive a threat is there. Always watch for strange behavior.

2. Recognize the threat and prepare your action plan.

3. Acquire the threat and immediately act on that plan. It usually becomes a case of fight or flight!

The Priorities of Survival

There is some merit to the principles listed below, but I find most of them a bit frivolous. Several of them are rather obvious to anyone who is concerned in any way with his survival in any situation. One exception here might be the combat mindset. Without combat mindset, survival in the face of any violent threat is a grim prospect at best. It is the cornerstone for all those concerned with their survival.

Stephen P. Wenger, in his book *Defensive Use of Firearms*, devotes space for his and Massad Ayoob's versions of the principles of survival. Much is made about each one's differences of opinion and who has more principles. It seems to be a war of semantics in the simplest sense. Here is what each is advocating:

Ayoob
1. Mental Awareness and Preparedness
2. Tactics
3. Skill
4. Choice of Equipment

Wenger
1. Mental Awareness
2. Mental Preparedness
3. Tactics
4. Skill
5. Choice of gear

So Ayoob has four principles and Wenger espouses five principles. Okay, but they are both stating the exact same thing. It really doesn't matter which of these lists you adopt. I do not have any heartburn with either of these lists, nor with the reason for their existence. It just appears to be a case of my list is bigger than yours!

Just for the record, here is my list:

1. Combat mindset
2. Training
3. Awareness (Color Code)
4. Choice of Gear

As stated before, I am keeping it simple by combining the states of mental awareness and preparedness into one: combat mindset. This mental awareness-preparedness stuff is fine, but it's redundant. One begets the other. Combat mindset is all-inclusive and covers any and all awareness and preparedness issues.

The Modern Technique of the Pistol

"The Modern Technique of the Pistol" was not a published book or paper by Col. Cooper, but rather a theme and a regimen that was instituted at Gunsite. Remember, Cooper formulated his Modern Technique as a direct result of his Big Bear, California, shooting events and the changes that evolved from the adoption of the combat techniques that he and his friends then used to compete with during these events. Cooper simply applied his Modern Technique principles to personal defense and began teaching these techniques at Gunsite.

When Cooper opened his school in Paulden, Arizona, in the late 1970s, the Modern Technique of the Pistol was the frontispiece of his Gunsite curriculum and still is. He taught the two-handed Weaver grip and stance with tactical movement and shooting. At the time, it was both new and a tremendous draw for Gunsite and Cooper himself. Col. Cooper became a "gun guru" and Gunsite grew and prospered. As far as I know, Cooper never put his Modern Techniques into writing but often verbally articulated them to many groups and to his students over the years. These techniques are, and I paraphrase:

1. Grip and Stance

The two-handed grip is the Weaver or the modified Weaver. Grip high on the handgun's tang with the index finger of the firing hand on the trigger halfway onto the first pad of the finger, firing-side thumb on top of the thumb safety, support-side thumb stacked next to the firing side thumb with no lateral pressure exerted on the thumb.

2. Body

It is erect, knees gently flexed, feet at a 30° angle to the target, isometric pressure on the frame with firing-side hand pushing forward, support-side hand pulling backward. Fingers over fingers (no support-side index finger resting on the front of the trigger guard). Support-side elbow pointing at the ground, firing-side elbow extended straight or slightly flexed, as desired.

3. Flash Sight Picture

Front sight remains inside outline of intended target area. With sufficient time, a focused sight picture should be attained.

4. Compressed Surprise Break

This is the action which causes the shot to break (fire) while the shooter is focused on the front sight alignment and picture and does not anticipate when the weapon will fire.

5. The Presentation

This is a kinesthetic (motion) response of the body to a stimulus (threat). The eye verifies sight alignment; the body does it in stance, aim, developing a kinesthetic stroke. Cooper always referred to the drawing of a weapon as a presentation. I refer to the presentation of the weapon as either the presentation or as the draw.

6. The Weapon

A heavy-duty autoloading pistol such as a .45 ACP 1911A1. If a revolver, it must be, at minimum, of .38 Special caliber.

Cooper's Principles of Personal Defense

In the late 1980s, Cooper put his thoughts on this subject in writing, in the form of a short book called *The Principles of Personal Defense.* He had founded Gunsite by then and wanted to advise the gun owning students and the public on his latest thoughts on the mental attitudes that must be inculcated in the mind of the student or gun owner during training in defensive guncraft techniques.

In *The Principles of Personal Defense,* Cooper states that there are seven principles or mental attitudes that the student must incorporate into his firearms training and which can affect his chances of being able to survive a potentially lethal gun fight. I consider all these to be elements of combat mindset.

Cooper's Seven Principles of Personal Defense are as follows:

1. Alertness
2. Decisiveness
3. Aggressiveness
4. Speed
5. Coolness
6. Ruthlessness
7. Surprise

These appear in no order of priority. They are all attitudes that you will maintain within yourself 24 hours of the day, seven days a week. In the event that a threatening situation comes your way, you will draw from the knowledge of these seven principles. They are not part and parcel of the Color Code of Mental Awareness, but rather dovetail nicely with its implementation into your daily life, especially if you carry a concealed weapon.

For example, imagine that you are in Condition Orange and very suspicious of a nearby individual who is sending all the wrong signals your way. Consciously you tell yourself you will act with speed and decisiveness should this person continue his overtly threatening manner towards you.

The Principles of Personal Defense consists of about 65 pages of Cooper's thoughts on the attitudes needed to survive the gun fight that you hope will never come your way. It is a modest-sized volume and one I would encourage all serious gun owners to read.

Cooper's The Principles of Personal Defense, published by Paladin Press.

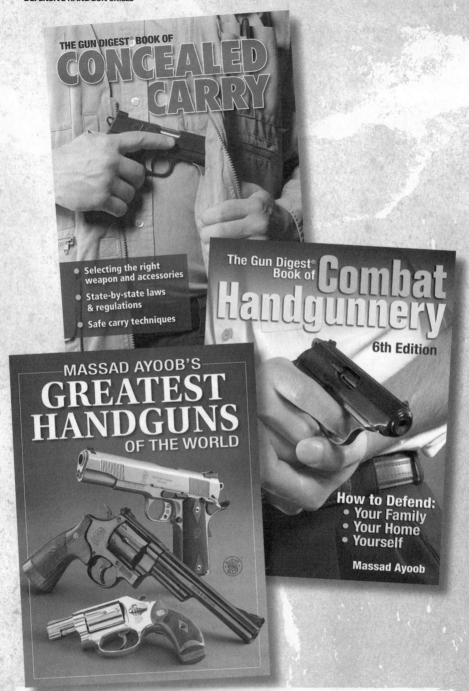

THE GUN DIGEST® BOOK OF
CONCEALED CARRY

- Selecting the right weapon and accessories
- State-by-state laws & regulations
- Safe carry techniques

The Gun Digest® Book of Combat Handgunnery
6th Edition

MASSAD AYOOB'S
GREATEST HANDGUNS
OF THE WORLD

How to Defend:
- Your Family
- Your Home
- Yourself

Massad Ayoob

Formerly affiliated with Lethal Force Institute and now director of the Massad Ayoob Group, best-selling author Massad Ayoob is an expert in handguns, defensive handgunning techniques and the justifiable use of force.

Chapter 5

Legal Considerations

The legal side of gun ownership is a veritable snakepit of good and bad. All gun owners need to take a crash course in the particulars of legal gun ownership in the state in which they reside. These statutes can vary from state to state – and sometimes from city to city – and it is incumbent on the individual gun owner to be well-versed on his local requirements for owning a firearm. A gun owner who is ignorant of these rules and regulations inevitably ends up getting crosswise with them, either unintentionally or intentionally. Most of us are conscientious law-bidding gun owners and play by all the rules.

Since I am not a lawyer and therefore not qualified to offer any legal advice on the subject of gun ownership and carrying a gun in public, I can only suggest that you consult with your attorney on this subject following a purchase of your first firearm. If you also have decided to apply for a concealed carry weapons permit (CCW), most respectable CCW classes have a portion of that class devoted to the legal responsibilities of concealed carry, usually taught by a retired or active duty law enforcement officer.

A knowledge of all the local statutes that govern firearms ownership will definitely affect the decisions you will make should you decide to carry a concealed weapon or even keep a gun in your home. When you couple this responsibility with your formal professional firearms training, you have built a solid base toward responsible, safe gun ownership, one that will minimize any legal problems for you and prevent any potential courtroom visits.

I would like to recommend a school that was formerly affiliated with Massad Ayoob, the Lethal Force Institute (LFI). It is located in Exeter, New Hampshire, and offers a heavy dose of education on the legal side of gun ownership and the use of lethal force in the protection of your life. LFI offers a Level I and Level II class in hand gun training. I strongly recommend attending one of these classes, if you are concerned about gun ownership and CCW carry laws in your state. The serious and conscientious gun owner will definitely benefit from having attended LFI, and its classes will complement any or all of your previous defensive handgun training.

Developing a proper Combat Mindset is an essential part of defensive guncraft.

Chapter 6

The Combat Mindset

Jeff Cooper said, "Mindset is everything, a willingness to take the step." What Cooper is referring to here by use of the word "step" is the gun owner's decision and willingness to use lethal force in the defense of his life. This is why I place Combat Mindset at the top of my priorities list.

At Front Sight Institute, with all our students we stressed the concept of Combat Mindset for the entire length of our handgun courses. In fact, it is the central theme of all firearms courses there. We stress it just as vigorously at my school as well. Every book worth its weight in paper and every firearms instructor I have ever spoken with all state that Combat Mindset is the engine that drives proper firearms training. This book concerns itself only with self-defense with the handgun, but the concept will apply to all weapons systems and their courses of instruction.

Aside from its overall effect that makes you want to win and succeed, Combat Mindset allows you to stay focused on your tasks and, if necessary, over-achieve. It lets you get the most out of every moment of your training and stay sharp. If you are working on your trigger control, for example, it allows you to think only about what you are doing at that precise moment in time and stay focused on each and every movement of the drill. Nothing else can disrupt your thought processes and get you off focus. However, if something is able to shake your concentration and you speed up your trigger press and drop a shot, you will instantly realize what has happened to cause your shot to fall out of the group. Simply take a deep breath, refocus on your trigger and trigger finger position and let the Combat Mindset kick back in before you commence your training drill. In our not-so-perfect world, you realize this will happen now and again. You shake it off and get back in the fight with the aid of your newly acquired Combat Mindset.

Cooper said that there is a direct link between Combat Mindset and marksmanship. I submit that this linkage can be traced to every segment of defensive guncraft. In the category of gun handling skills, it can produce the desire to dry-practice for hours at a time and, most importantly, the passion to push yourself to the next level of proficiency with your weapon. It is what pushes a student to invest the time and money to acquire the highest ranking he can achieve with his or her weapon of choice, that of Combat Master. It takes months and months of dry practice, live fire, and then passing a grueling and arduous range test to acquire this most prestigious of rankings.

Jeff Cooper further added, "Obviously, if you are a good shot your self-confidence takes care of itself. You don't have to worry about it." He also said, "Far more important than brilliant pistol craft is attitude. The state of mind to do what is needful when the time arises." The best shot in the world is helpless if he or she doesn't want to shoot. From a fine-tuned Combat Mindset arises this proper attitude and technique.

With an active and well-groomed Combat Mindset, you will find yourself accomplishing feats with your handgun that you could never imagine yourself accomplishing prior to the start of your training. A part of this fine-tuned mindset is the realization that you are capable of taking the step that Cooper referred to. Your mindset is *I am ready and capable of protecting my family and myself should the need ever arise.* Counter to that, you are also supremely hopeful that you never have to showcase your newly-acquired talents.

Many times at Front Sight, I have started out with a brand-new, never-fired-a-gun-before student. He would literally be shaking in his boots in total fear of what he had signed up to learn. With a lot of gentle instruction and a huge dose of stressing that he adopt a Combat Mindset toward his training drills, he would gradually lose his self-imposed fear of this training; it would be replaced with an air of confidence at his achievements as his learning curve was going off the charts. Then when the course was completed, he would come to me and say, "I cannot believe what I have learned here and how glad and happy I am to have experienced this type of training." Just a sample of Combat Mindset at work.

The other benefit of Combat Mindset is the confidence that it instills in you on a daily basis, especially if you have spent a considerable amount of time on the Failure to Stop drill. For those of you new to defensive handgun training and self-defense techniques, the Failure to Stop drill is a firearms exercise that incorporates a head shot that, if fired properly, will inflict lethal force on the recipient. It prepares you for the possibility that, when you are engaged in a gunfight and the two shots you have fired into the thoracic cavity of the

When you have fully developed a Combat Mindset, your every move will be well-rehearsed and reflexive – even when reacting to a potentially disastrous malfunction such as this stovepipe failure.

assailant have not stopped his violent attack on you. a third shot to the head may be necessary.

Placement of the first two shots should be to the aggressor's thoracic cavity to terminate his attack. However, while under attack, you cannot depend on these two shots stopping the assailant, especially if he is on drugs, is drunk or is wearing body armor. Your controlled pair of shots may have put the assailant on the ground, but if he is still standing and brandishing his weapon, a head shot is now your only option, unless you choose to flee the scene. Firing what we call a head shot or, clinically, a cranio-ocular shot is your last option to stop the fight.

The thought of terminating another human's life can be daunting prospect, and not all victims are prepared to undertake this necessity. So how are we able to achieve this mental state that will lead to our making the decision to terminate a violent assailant when our own life is in danger? With hundreds and hundreds of hours of dry practice. Developing your technique, confidence and speed, you will simultaneously develop the reflexive mindset to take the step and survive a threat to your life. With hundreds of hours on the range and in shoot houses, shooting at hostage targets and bad guy targets, you will develop a natural reflexive reaction to the threat. Autopilot will kick in and the shot will be taken.

Another phenomenon of Combat Mindest is called "going inside the bubble," a term I credit to the late GSGT. Carlos Hathcock, USMC, a legendary Vietnam sniper. "Going inside the bubble" was his term for blocking out everything in his world for the moment it took to concentrate on pressing the trigger for that 1000-yard sniper shot he was about to take. With hundreds of hours of dry practice, you will gradually acquire the ability to execute the shot or shots while on autopilot. Just like Hathcock, you will go inside the bubble and take that precision pistol shot to stop the lethal attack on your person. If you do, you will survive the gunfight and live to be with your family, confident in your skills and knowing full well that Combat Mindset was instrumental in getting you there.

Lawrence's Combat Triad

In Eric Lawrence's excellent book *The Operator's Tactical Pistol Shooting Manual*, he devotes an entire chapter to an explanation of the concept of the Combat Triad and its place in defensive gun craft. It is a concept that has its roots in the US military and helps the student to identify, assess and respond to any number of potential life-threatening scenarios. It consists of three sides of a triangle. The right side of the triangle represents the principles of Gun Handling; the left side represents the principles of Marksmanship; and the base represents Mindset.

A knowledge and understanding of the concept of the Combat Triad will aid the student in developing a doctrinal foundation that will allow him or her to be able to identify, assess and respond rapidly and with precision to any potential threat encountered out on the street.

Paraphrasing Mr. Lawrence:

Gun handling: The ability to safely and confidently manipulate and responsibly handle your weapon/firearm through any and all procedures, for example, unloading and loading, all reload drills, malfunction clearances, chamber checking and the presentation (draw).

Marksmanship: Controlling sight alignment and sight picture perfectly while performing precision trigger control to achieve consistent, rapid and accurate hits on your intended target.

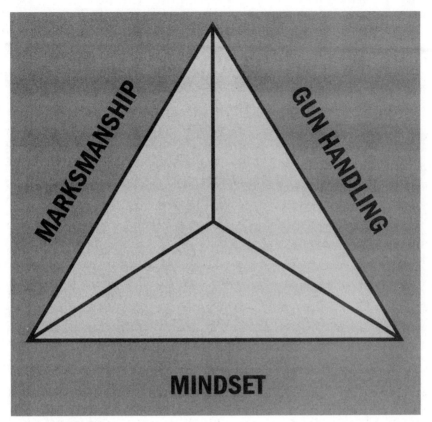

Author's Combat Triad.

Mindset: A form of mental conditioning that enables the student or shooter to survive a lethal encounter. Mindset also facilitates the student's desire to train to the highest level of handgun skill he or she is capable of attaining and greatly improves his or her chances of survivability in the face of imminent danger.

In closing, there is a well-known axiom in our business that goes like this: "Train as you would fight and you will fight as you have trained."

Comfort of Skill at Arms

Comfort of Skill at Arms is truly a state of mind that becomes more and more evident as your training intensifies and your gains in confidence overtake you. As your training intensifies and your marksmanship skills, gun handling and mindset grow, you will become aware of a strong aura of pride and a comfort in your new abilities. You now feel that you are in charge of your own self-protection and you feel good about this transformation.

The confident feeling known as Comfort of Skill at Arms is a result of the complete mastery of your chosen weapon.

When you arrive at this mental plateau, you have achieved what is called the Comfort of Skill at Arms. It is a very rewarding and wonderfully confident state of mind that justifies your efforts to master all the skills needed to handle your firearm safely and with precision. It is a unique feeling, one which no one has to tell you that you've acquired. You will be very aware of this feeling and the difference in your attitude toward firearms. To sum it up: it is an extremely positive feeling. It is also a pride in your performance with firearms today, as opposed to your first day on the range. Your level of expertise, training, proficiency and upbeat enthusiasm are obvious to you and all those you come in contact with. Basically, the more center of mass hits you make, with consistency, the more you know you will be able to make them when it matters the most!

Five Categories of Mindset

From the sublime to the ridiculous, or rather the opposite! Here is a ranking and grading system for the student as he or she sets out on his or her firearms training. It also is an indicator of the student's mindset during this training. There are five categories of mindset that serve to identify the shooter's level of proficiency. They are as follows:

Intentionally Incompetent (II)

The person has no idea about his or her condition, nor does he or she care about training and has no desire to improve his or her skills. He or she is a danger to bystanders, and one should not waste any time trying to help or encourage him or her.

Unintentionally Incompetent (UI)

Unaware of not knowing how to perform the required gun handling tasks correctly. He or she exhibits a mindset that indicates that he or she could learn the basic gun handling skills, if he or she tried. Simply put, he or she does not know how much he or she does not know!

Consciously Incompetent (CI)

The student is aware of his or her need to learn one or more basic gun handling tasks.

Consciously Competent (CC)

He or she is able to perform basic gun handling tasks when consciously thinking about these tasks.

Unconsciously competent (UC)

With training, the student is able to perform all the firearm tasks without conscious thought. This is the autopilot concept of gun handling.

One thing to remember: we all started out as a UI with our introduction to firearms and shooting. As we train hard and seek professional training, most of us will improve our skills and consciously become more proficient and lose the UI label.

The OODA Loop

Another defensive guncraft concept is one conceived by Air Force Col. John Boyd. He was a Korean War Ace fighter pilot and the USAF's resident thinker. He was called "40 Second Boyd" by his fellow pilots for his ability to shoot down a North Korean fighter plane within 40 seconds, using his loop: he claimed he could maneuver from a position of disadvantage (enemy on his tail) to a position of advantage (on the enemy's tail) in 40 seconds or less.

While thinking about his many aerial duals with MIG fighter planes, Boyd became aware that his response to a MIG attack was always the same and nearly always successful. What Boyd came up with was his concept called the "OODA

Loop." During his fights, he actually performed an aerial loop, gained the advantage by attacking from the rear, and shot down his opponent in mere seconds. As a result of his aerial successes, he formulated what became known as the OODA (Observe, Orient, Decide and Act) Loop. In flight school, Col. Boyd taught and promoted his OODA Loop concept and its application to aerial combat and it received widespread acceptance from his students. Col. Boyd went on to a career in the US government service and continued to promote his OODA Loop concept in various fields of endeavor.

In Boyd's view, any conflict could be viewed as a duel wherein each adversary observes (O) his opponent's actions, orients (O) himself to the unfolding situation, decides (D) on the most appropriate response or counter response, then acts (A) on that decision. The competitor who moves through the OODA Loop cycle the fastest gained the ultimate advantage by disrupting his enemy's ability to respond effectively.

Boyd's OODA Loop theory does have some room for acceptance in the shooting fraternity, where it has gained some ground beyond its origin as a technique of aerial warfare. When considered in the context of defensive handgun and concealed carry training, it fits well.

> ***"Mindset is everything...***
> ***a willingness to take the step."***
>
> *Lt Col. Jeff Cooper.*

Chapter 7

Weapons and Gear

A detailed discussion of this subject would likely cover about several chapters of text, so rather than launch into something of that sort, I will keep it simple.

In my school, we take a bit of time to engage in a brief lecture on many of the weapons, holsters and accessories from which you can select and that will cover the broadest base of common appeal to the average student. We do spend a lot of time on concealed carry equipment, so that those students interested in applying for a permit get a chance to learn about their options in this area.

Small-Bore vs. Big-Bore

For the selection of a concealed carry weapon, many instructors will advise their students to purchase a .22 Long Rifle pistol and train up to a larger caliber firearm. The thinking here is that the student will adjust to the lower noise, recoil and shock of this smaller caliber handgun and will eventually be comfortable enough to move up to the larger caliber pistol with ease.

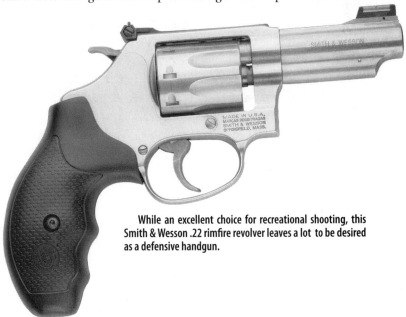

While an excellent choice for recreational shooting, this Smith & Wesson .22 rimfire revolver leaves a lot to be desired as a defensive handgun.

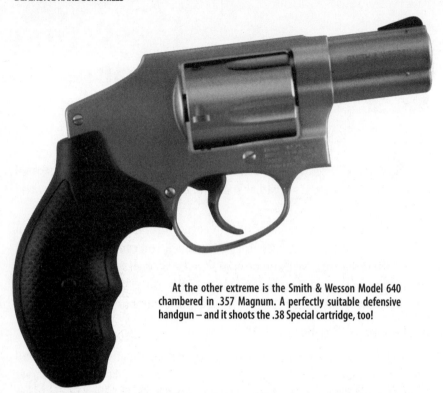

At the other extreme is the Smith & Wesson Model 640 chambered in .357 Magnum. A perfectly suitable defensive handgun – and it shoots the .38 Special cartridge, too!

I view this as a colossal waste of time and money. I prefer to advise my students to bring a .38 Special revolver or 9mm, .40 S&W, .38 Super or .45 ACP semiautomatic to start the class. We teach the student how to properly and safely control and manage the recoil and push of the weapon, even when firing the multiple target drill. This is done with the application of proper stance and grip instruction in an acceptable period of time, usually just a few hours. Students quickly become very confident with their marksmanship and gun handling skills. Any concerns about noise and recoil quickly are forgotten. I've taught many women without any prior firearms training or experience how to shoot a Glock Model 23 in .40 S&W with ease and precision, and after several hours they have openly thanked me for insisting that they start out with the weapon that will, in all likelihood, end up being their carry weapon.

Revolver or Semiauto?

The first decision you must make is whether to carry a revolver or a semi-automatic pistol. If it is a revolver, select a manufacturer that produces a rugged and reliable double action model. Ruger and Smith & Wesson are excellent selections. Both are top-line companies with numerous high-quality models in .38 Special caliber.

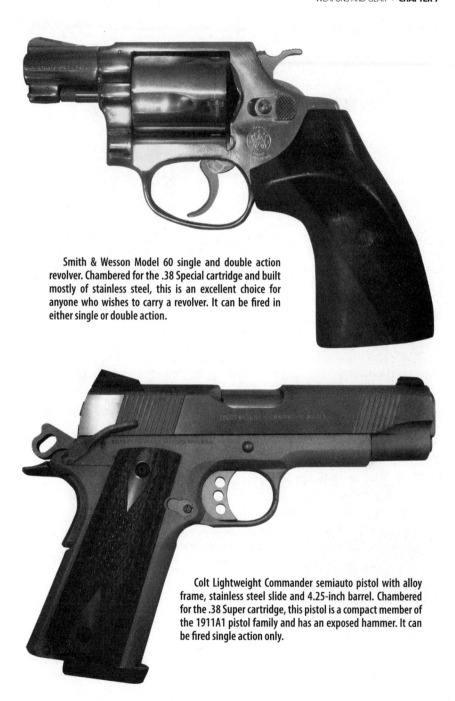

Smith & Wesson Model 60 single and double action revolver. Chambered for the .38 Special cartridge and built mostly of stainless steel, this is an excellent choice for anyone who wishes to carry a revolver. It can be fired in either single or double action.

Colt Lightweight Commander semiauto pistol with alloy frame, stainless steel slide and 4.25-inch barrel. Chambered for the .38 Super cartridge, this pistol is a compact member of the 1911A1 pistol family and has an exposed hammer. It can be fired single action only.

Chambered for the .40 Smith & Wesson cartridge, the Glock Model 23 is a fairly compact semiauto pistol that can be fired in double action only. It has a polymer frame, 4-inch barrel, no manual safeties and no external hammer.

The Kahr Arms K40 is a compact semiauto pistol that can be fired in double action only. Chambered for the .40 Smith & Wesson cartridge, it has a stainless steel slide and frame, a 3.5-inch barrel, no manual safeties and no external hammer.

Stay with a stainless steel version. This type of gun resists the formation of surface rust and is easy to clean and maintain. Because you will be carrying the weapon close to your body, under clothing, body heat and perspiration will easily encourage the formation of surface rust on blued firearms. The cleaning of a stainless steel weapon is easy and simple.

Select a 4-inch-barreled model as a compromise between potential accuracy and ease of carry. Depending on the caliber and frame size, the weapon will have a capacity of either five or six rounds. You will want to investigate the need for a speed loader to assist in having extra ammunition capacity and the ability to rapidly reload the weapon.

For the semiautomatic enthusiast, I recommend that you examine any of dozens of models by several manufacturers in the calibers of 9mm, .40 S&W, .38 Super or .45 ACP. Any of the above is more than suitable, provided the shooter uses a cartridge with jacketed hollowpoint or frangible (i.e., easily fragmented) bullet of the type usually referred to as self defense ammunition.

I would recommend that the student limit his or her search and analysis to Glock and any of several 1911A1 type manufacturers: Springfield Armory, Kimber, Para Ordnance, Dan Wesson, Colt and Wilson Combat, just to name a few. Quality, accuracy and reliability is always a consideration in this type of gun, along with price. All of these firearms meet that criterion, but my concern for any concealed carry or duty weapon is that it is very easy to deploy into action. The Glocks and 1911Al meet that need.

The Glock is the easiest of all weapons to operate. It is essentially a "point and shoot" firearm. Simply load it, point it at your target and press the trigger; it always goes bang! All of the Glock's safety devices are internal and operate off the movement of the trigger mechanism. A new student without prior experience can be quickly brought up to speed with this firearm and become totally comfortable carrying, shooting and operating it.

The single action 1911A1s are a bit more complex to operate but still offer a good degree of simplicity for the new student. The 1911A1 has two external safety devices: a thumb safety and a grip safety. The thumb safety is located on the upper left side of the frame. The grip safety is a part of the backstrap and is located at the upper rear of the frame. Both of these safeties must be depressed before the weapon will fire.

In many of the late model 1911A1s, several manufacturers have designed and installed into their weapons a passive firing pin safety. It operates off the movement of the trigger and is therefore not a technique that the shooter has to be directly concerned with, other than to be sure that he or she fully depresses the trigger. The firing pin safety simply drops out of the way and allows the firing pin, when struck by the hammer, to move forward and strike the rear face of the primer. I feel that the firing pin safety device is a good feature to have on any semiautomatic pistol. Here again, teaching a new student to safely and correctly fire these weapons is not a major problem for either the student or the instructor in regard to the passive firing pin safety.

Many companies now make 1911-type semiauto pistols, but the full-size "Government Models" shown here are perhaps a bit too bulky for daily defensive use. The more compact "Commander"-size 1911 is usually a better chcoice.

Both of these styles of guns come in either 3.5-, 4.25- or 5-inch barrel lengths. If a concealed carry weapon is the objective in your training, I recommend the purchase of a 4.25-inch-barreled "Commander"-sized model (named after the Colt Commander, the first gun of its type), as a compromise between weight, carry and accuracy objectives. If marksmanship or competition is an objective of the student, then a 5-inch model will serve better.

As I mentioned earlier, due to the stress and anxiety induced by even the threat of a pending lethal encounter, you need to be able to bring to bear the simplest weapon system available. Remember, in this moment, all your simple motor skills degrade. Your ability to perform the simplest of tasks becomes very difficult. Having to deal with the proper sequence of pushing various levers and buttons can be virtually impossible. Forget dealing with a horrendous double action trigger pull. In a moment of peril, all this can be a daunting task. With considerable dry practice and live fire, a shooter can train up to learn how to deal with a complex weapon and develop a degree of confidence with it. It is just easier and requires less time to train with a Glock or 1911A1. When the "flag goes up," your chance of getting it right and surviving the gunfight is simply greater with a semiauto.

Parts Nomenclature, Typical Single/Double Action
Revolver (S&W M60 Shown)

1. Cylinder
2. Front sight
3. Muzzle
4. Frame
5. Trigger guard
6. Trigger
7. Stock panel

8. Frontstrap
9. Backstrap
10. Hammer
11. Cylinder release
12. Crane
13. Ejector rod

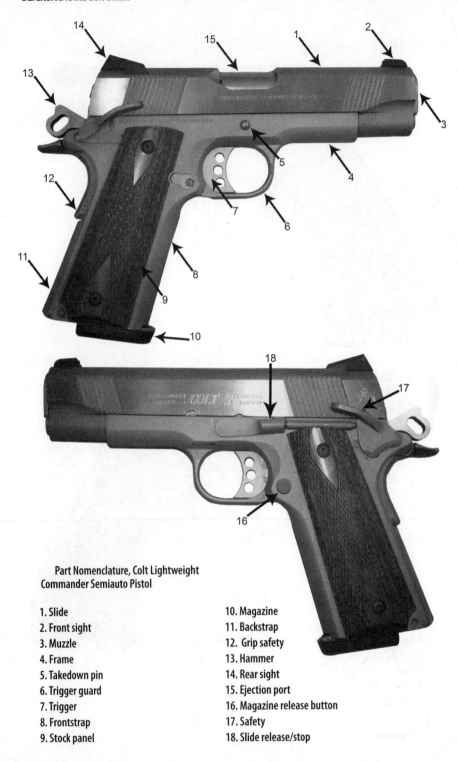

Part Nomenclature, Colt Lightweight
Commander Semiauto Pistol

1. Slide
2. Front sight
3. Muzzle
4. Frame
5. Takedown pin
6. Trigger guard
7. Trigger
8. Frontstrap
9. Stock panel

10. Magazine
11. Backstrap
12. Grip safety
13. Hammer
14. Rear sight
15. Ejection port
16. Magazine release button
17. Safety
18. Slide release/stop

Parts Nomenclature, Glock Model 23 Semiauto Pistol

1. Slide
2. Front sight
3. Muzzle
4. Frame
5. Trigger guard
6. Trigger safety
7. Trigger
8. Frontstrap
9. Stock panel
10. Magazine
11. Backsttrap
12. Rear sight
13. Ejection port
14. Takedown lever
15. Slide stop
16. Magazine release button

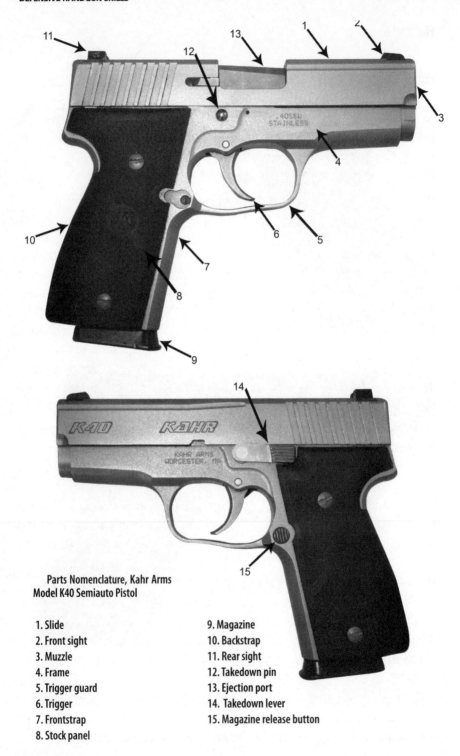

**Parts Nomenclature, Kahr Arms
Model K40 Semiauto Pistol**

1. Slide
2. Front sight
3. Muzzle
4. Frame
5. Trigger guard
6. Trigger
7. Frontstrap
8. Stock panel

9. Magazine
10. Backstrap
11. Rear sight
12. Takedown pin
13. Ejection port
14. Takedown lever
15. Magazine release button

Holsters

In the arena of holster wear, the choices are numerous and mistakes can be made easily.

Do not buy the least expensive holster! Limit your search to high-quality leather or Kydex style holsters. Kydex is a brand name for a polymer plastic compound holster that is thermoplastically formed in a mold and assembled with screws or rivets. There are several companies that market a Kydex holster. Blade Tech has the largest market share, followed closely by Uncle Mike's, Fobus, KyTac and Side Armor. There are several styles, models and prices from each manufacturer.

The Kydex holster is a rigid, stable holster that allows easy, safe and rapid presentation and re-holstering of the weapon. It is not affected by water, humidity or temperature changes. The Kydex holster comes in drop and offset drop configurations. A drop model holster is one that has the pouch of the holster hanging directly below the gun belt. An offset drop is offset away from the belt hanger between the belt and pouch. The offset model was originally designed for female shooters whose anatomy differs from that of the male. The offset kept the pouch more vertical and the grip frame away from the shooter's waist.

Currently the offset holster is the most popular model and is much in demand by male and female shooters alike. As a user of Kydex holsters, I urge the shooter to buy an offset drop model.

One disadvantage to the Kydex holsters is that they are model specific. Because they are molded to the image of the weapon, only one model of weapon will fit in anyone holster. I own five Kydex holsters for the weapons I train with and carry.

I also carry a Model 60 shot 2-1/2-inch .38 Special revolver in a Blocker Inside the Waist Band (IWB) holster. It is made of leather with a metal-reinforced opening for one handed re-holstering. It is very comfortable, light and easy to wear in any type of weather year around. For my 1911A1 Commander, I wear a simple leather belt hip holster Outside the Waist Band (OWB) for my firing side.

Stay away from any holster made from a soft suede or other flimsy ballistic nylon. Their price is attractive, but their performance is wanting! They both tend to collapse during re-holstering and require the use of the support-side hand to assist during this procedure. It also requires more time to accomplish re-holstering.

In summation, there is no one-size-fits-all solution to the selection of a concealed carry weapon holster system. Clothing, weather conditions, work or social occasions all influence your final choices of gear and equipment. Caliber, firepower and stopping power will also have some impact on your decision.

A selection of weapons and essential gear. Clockwise from upper right: Colt 1911A1 semiauto pistol with holster, magazine pouch and spare magazine; Glock semiauto pistol with spare magazine; folding tactical-style drop-point knife with belt clip; Mace pepper spray; Kahr Arms semiauto pistol with extra

magazine; serrated-blade folding knife; Smith & Wesson Model 60 single/double action revolver with speedloader and holster. Center: Blackberry cellphone and LED tactical flashlight.

One last comparison to assist you in your selection of the best CCW weapon for your carry or "bedside" needs goes as follows:

Revolver	Semiautomatic
• Safer and easier to hide	• More compact
• Easily operated	• Easier to clean
	• More firepower
	• Faster cycle speed
	• Faster reloading time

In the Home

For a bedside gun, none of the above suggestions is really a consideration. It mostly gets down to your preferred brand of gun, caliber and firepower preferences. Actually, a 12 gauge pump shotgun fits the purpose very well!

In regard to revolver accessories, I have already mentioned the need for a speedloader for the enhancement of speed and firepower of your revolver. For a semiautomatic, two spare loaded magazines are needed. One item of note here: do not load the magazines to full capacity. A fully-loaded eight-round magazine will more than likely have too much upward pressure against the base of the slide/bolt and thus induce a possible malfunction of your weapon – not something you want to deal with in a possible lethal encounter!

Finally, note that a small LED flashlight is an excellent addition to your gear, along with a cell phone, pepper spray and a high-quality folding knife.

Chapter 8

Training

As I have stated in previous chapters, the most common sin committed by prospective gun owners who wish to purchase a handgun for personal protection is to buy the gun, take it to a gun range and load up a couple of rounds in it, fire them at a paper target and go home and secure the gun in their nightstand or gun safe. They believe they are all "tuned up" for the robber, should he attempt a home invasion in the middle of the night.

Such people are sadly mistaken. Unfortunately, this is often the rule rather than the exception. Remember what I said about the deterioration of the fine motor skills during times of extreme stress, fear and anxiety? They vanish instantly, and simple tasks like reaching to open a drawer in your dresser top become very difficult. It is during a response to a threat that very bad things will happen, things that can affect the outcome and determine whether you survive in this situation. Even if you have trained diligently for this moment and your reflexive training takes over, you will find these life-saving techniques difficult to perform under the stress this threat to you generates. It all goes to the question, "If you have never performed this feat, how are you going to be able to accomplish it when the well-known substance hits the fan?"

If you are at all serious about your personal protection and your ability to survive a possible gunfight, you need to have undergone a minimum of 50 hours of professional firearms instruction at one of the better-known training schools anywhere in the country, soon after the purchase of your firearm. Fifty hours constitutes a lengthy four-day class or a week-long class at any of several schools.

Now, let's talk about the type of school you should be looking into. As an example, if you were looking to learn to drive a racecar would you be looking at a school that offers a course in how to drive heavy equipment? Of course not. Same with firearms training: you should be looking for a school that offers a two- or four-day defensive handgun course in its curriculum. There are many fine schools out there with an excellent staff of instructors on them, but you need to investigate their backgrounds. Many former Green Berets, SEALs, law enforcement officers and competitive shooters have founded excellent training schools, but what do they teach? That which they know best. Therefore they cater to military, law enforcement departments and competitive shooters. Just seems right, doesn't it? They teach a lot of CQB (close quarters battle) techniques, advanced tactics and other martial techniques that will be too advanced for the average new gun owner or beginning shooter.

Remember, look for the defensive handgun classes in their curriculum before applying. After you have completed your two- and four-day defensive handgun course, you will be prepared to take one of these advanced tactical courses, if your interests take you in that direction. You will have a firm, basic foundation of understanding in defensive handgun techniques upon which to build.

The Basics

In your four-day defensive handgun course you should be taught, and should develop, a mastery of chamber checking, unloading and loading, stance and grip, after-action drills, the presentation, malfunction drills, and Failure to Stop drills. Home Invasion scenarios and Shoot House exercises should also be part of any good curriculum. Practicing shooting multiple targets, range commands, range safety, night shooting and a good dose of basic marksmanship techniques will enable you to consistently get good hits on the target and will round out your training. In addition, many schools have, as part of the four-day course, an entire afternoon devoted to shooting from concealment.

Dry Practice

Apart from all this good stuff in the class, you will gain an appreciation for the merits of setting up a strict weekly dry practice regimen, so as to not lose the edge on the skills you have worked so hard to attain while attending the

Dry practice – practicing various drills with an unloaded gun – is the best way to build familiarity with your chosen weapon.

class. Dry practice is the method by which you continue to hone your newly acquired skills and elevate them to the next level.

Dry practice means going through the drill strokes of a given gun handling technique with an empty firearm (emphasis on the "empty" part)! You would of course perform several chamber checks and remove the magazine and any and all ammunition from your dry practice area, prior to starting your dry practice sessions. For the serious handgunner, dry practice will program your future response to a possible life-threatening situation. Cooper often stated, "Your shooting is a programmed reflex and you program it only by familiarity."

There are several instructors who believe and teach instinctive or point shooting. It consists of drawing and shooting from the hip or, at best, in a crouched position with the weapon extended a short distance from the body. The shooter does not acquire a sight picture. In all honesty, this may be your only option for survival, if the adversary is within approximately three meters and obviously intends you serious harm. If you have the opportunity, however, get that front sight in focus and take two well-aimed thoracic cavity shots to stop his attack. Dry practice builds the ability to perform this kind of response during your moment of great peril.

Following your scheduled school classwork, you should start a strict dry practice schedule. First, select a quiet, private and safe location to conduct this training. It must be located away from family or friends and should have a solid backstop for target location. In many cases, this may be a basement area in your home. Use a 3x5-inch card and paint about a 2-inch solid black circle in the center of it. This will be your point of aim. Mark a spot on the floor approximately 5 meters from the wall to which the card is taped. This will be your training distance from the target.

Remember, in defensive handgun aiming techniques, you are aiming at the center of that dot. We refer to it as shooting center of mass, as opposed to a six o'clock hold, which one does when shooting at greater distances. After you have completed your dry practice, remove the target from view. No need to tempt a passerby or other family member to try his hand at dry practice, only to touch off a negligent discharge in the process. Your sessions should last no longer than 15 minutes in duration, twice a week. Beyond that amount of time, you will get tired and lose focus. Here, it is a case of the law of diminishing returns: you are practicing imperfect techniques and rather than engrain the wrong procedures, it is better to simply stop your session, hopefully on a high note.

You should also confine your sessions to practicing just one segment or technique at a time. If you are practicing sight alignment and you feel that after 10 minutes of practice you are definitely on top of your game, then you may

Performed at the right time and in a separate session, trigger control is an essential part of dry practice.

decide to call an end to this session. No need to get tired and lose the edge you have gained at this point. Remember, engraining one procedure at a time is what develops the reflexive nature of your techniques.

Also, do not try to dry practice your trigger control at this point simply because you feel you still need another five minutes of training. Save the trigger control work for your next session. Fifteen minutes of trigger control dry practice is going to bring faster results than squeezing in five minutes of possibly marginal dry practice on the same technique. Trying to force your training just because you feel you owe yourself the time may be more counter productive than you realize. A better answer to this is to set up a controlled and planned regimen with a system of stops to evaluate your progress along the way. Don't worry; as you advance through your training, you will become very aware of your progress and downfalls and will know immediately if any changes are needed to set you back on the right course. You then become your own instructor!

Regarding the speed of your sessions, start out slowly. Learn the mechanics of each technique or motion. Engrain them in your technique so you do not have to consciously think out each step, as you will at the start. When you are confident that you understand the mechanics of each technique, then the speed will begin to appear with each repetition. This will occur naturally. Do not attempt to consciously speed these moves up. If you do, you will more than likely get out of sequence and tempo and all the wheels will come off your practice session and you will need to start over again. Speed comes only after mechanics and tempo (smoothness) have been engrained. Don't worry, you will have plenty of time to attain that blinding speed you have seen in the movies or TV – which, by the way, is more a product of editing than it is of the actor's ability.

Dry Practice: A Typical Session

We will now run through a simulation of an actual dry practice session as it might be conducted by a student. First, set up your area for practice and remove ALL ammunition from the room. You will use no blanks, snap caps, empty casings or other forms of dummy rounds. No ammunition! You will have no magazines in the room, as well.

Chamber check your weapon several times, until you are absolutely convinced that you are handling an empty weapon. Now, say out loud, "I am starting my dry practice session." Establish, in your mind, what you wish to practice and begin your drill. You may chamber check your weapon from time to time to reinforce in your mind that the weapon remains empty. This is good for your focus and confidence while you practice.

Again, you will not have any magazines available during your sessions. This gives pause to semiautomatic owners who wish to dry practice with guns that have an onboard magazine safety feature that requires a magazine in place to allow the weapon to cycle and the trigger to operate. In these sessions, you will need to set up a procedure for using an EMPTY magazine for those techniques that require you to cycle your slide in order to complete your practice session.

> ### "It is better to have a gun and not need it, than it is to need a gun and not have it."
>
> *Dr. "Naish" Piazza Front Sight, Nevada 2001*

It is important that once you have completed these drills that you remove the magazine from the room. Another option is to plan your dry practice session to run those techniques that require a magazine to be used for just that one practice time. That way you can stay focused on the drills and not have to include a magazine in any of the other sessions.

When you are satisfied with your progress or have been doing it for the prescribed amount of time, then say "Stop" out loud. Then add, "My dry practice is now over." Chamber check your weapon and safely store it away. Remove your target from the wall and double check the room to be sure there is no remaining evidence of your dry practice activities.

Live Fire Practice

Let's discuss the live fire activity that should accompany your dry practice. I recommend that you go to your favorite range twice a month. You should not fire more than 50 rounds through your weapon at any of these sessions. You are only shooting to validate your dry practice progress. You are no longer a recreational shooter! Do not dump a magazine into the target. Do not stray from your training schedule and shoot any exercise that you have not dry practiced. As just stated, you are simply validating, with live fire, what you have engrained and mastered through your dry practice. Fifty rounds is sufficient to accomplish this and give you insight into your progress. If you revert to your past range mentality practices, you will undo all the progress gained in the dry practice sessions and begin to backslide in your training.

There is a saying among teachers in this business that goes, "Shooting is bad for shooting." You should no longer be thinking of yourself as a recreational plinker, but rather a combat shooter who is in training to program your response for that lethal encounter that we all hope will never happen.

Keep in mind that your dry practice to live fire ratio should now be 80% dry practice to 20% live fire. You should consciously work at maintaining this ratio. It will keep your techniques razor-sharp and your training curve on an upward trend.

Imagination helps a lot when you are dry practicing. I have said before, no ammunition or magazines are to be present during dry practice. So how can you practice your techniques without these devices around? You can use pen caps and thimbles for the empty shell casings in the malfunction clearance drills. Pantomime all the reloading drills by simply moving your hands through the strokes to complete the motion.

For the tactical reload drill, use no weapon. Accomplish the movement with empty magazines. Your hands should move in the prescribed manner to replicate the drill, as you would do on the range. All of this accomplishes the results of engraining the movements of the drill without introducing the potential for danger and risk of injuries that a negligent discharge brings.

As your training intensifies and your gun handling, confidence and accuracy soar, you will begin to feel a strong sense of pride in your accomplishments, not to mention an awareness that you are definitely in charge of your own self-protection. When this sense permeates your every minute of training, you have achieved that feeling we referred to earlier, the Comfort of Skill at Arms. It is a very rewarding and wonderful feeling that gives justification to your efforts at mastering the skills of the handgun.

Chapter 9

Unloading and Loading the Handgun

These techniques involve the physical act of altering the status of a particular weapon. Unloading and loading start and end with a chamber check – without fail!

Unloading

Semiautomatics

Thumb safety off. Thumb back the hammer.

Put the safety on and remove the magazine and place it in an empty pocket.

If a round is in the chamber, put the safety off, muzzle pointed downrange. Holding the weapon in your firing-side hand, rotate it 90° to the horizontal, form a large cup with your palm of your support-side hand and place it over the ejection port.

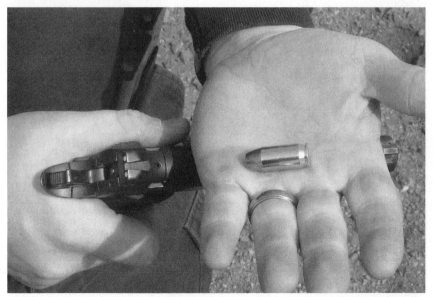

With the muzzle facing downrange, elevate it slightly and press the slide slowly to the rear and let the ejected round fall into your hand. Stow the round in a pocket and perform another chamber check. Put the safety on.

Revolvers

Simply perform the standard chamber check procedure and press back on the ejector rod to unload all the chambers in the cylinder.

Loading

Semiautomatics

"Wedge" chamber check method.

Safety on. Insert a fully loaded magazine.

Safety off. Rack the slide briskly to the rear with your support-side hand, release it and let it go forward under it own spring tension.

Your support-side hand should make contact with your firing-side shoulder to ensure that you have released the slide completely and have not eased it forward. Easing the slide forward with the support-side hand may induce a malfunction.

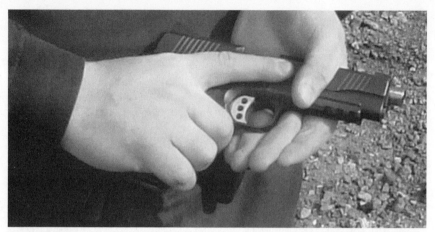

Perform another chamber check with the safety off. Then safety on and either holster your weapon or stand by at the ready position.

Revolvers

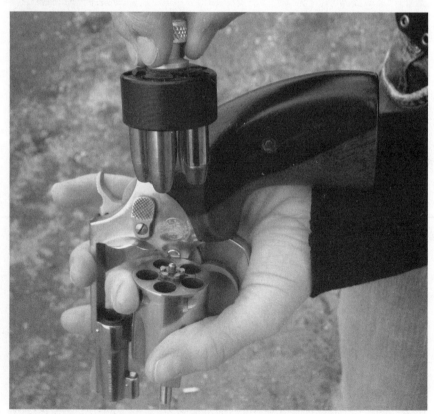

Perform the standard chamber check, leaving the cylinder in the open position. Use a speed loader or load individual rounds into each chamber.

Check to be sure all chambers are full

and close the cylinder.

In the Ready Position, the weapon's safety can be on, if the situation dictates. It is normally is off, at the beginning. Your arms and weapon are positioned at a 45° angle to the ground.

The Ready Position

The Ready Position is an alert or standby position. You can observe, as-sess a situation or await a range command while in this position. Your trigger finger is off the trigger and at home base.

From the Ready Position, the shooter can go to any other gun handling position.

Chapter 11

The Grip

During the research for and writing of this book, it became evident to me that a chapter was needed to cover the subject of the grip. I have read whatever articles I could find about the subject and have had numerous pro and con discussions on this subject with many individuals. I have even experimented with and developed my own iteration of the modified Weaver grip system, best suited for defensive and self protection scenarios. Where I have introduced this Aggressive Modified Weaver grip (AMW) to new students, the response and reception to it has been very encouraging and has met with much approval.

Of course, as we've mentioned, the Weaver grip owes its existence to Deputy Jack Weaver of the L.A. county sheriff's dept. and his days at the Lake Arrowhead, California, competitive shoots with Col. Jeff Cooper in the '50s and '60s. Since then it has undergone a few modifications, not the least of which are mine!

The grip is the manner in which a shooter initially holds his weapon if he or she intends to discharge it. But grip is more important and critical to proper shooting techniques than merely providing a means of holding and firing the weapon. It is the conduit through which the shooter transmits images and actions from his brain to his trigger finger. While this is occurring, the grip must be perfectly in place and ready to respond to additional commands. The selection and mastering of this perfect grip is essential to the achieving of consistent and accurate defensive shooting.

The Thumb Over Thumb Grip.

Let's examine the various grip systems available to today's shooters. We will go into detail on each and wind up with a detailed discussion of the grip that I espouse, recommend and currently teach.

The Thumb Over Thumb Grip

The first grip we will examine is the simplest one to learn and use. It is called the Thumb Over Thumb Grip and is considered the basic entry-level grip that I recommend for new students and beginners to pistol shooting. It affords comfort and will allow the student to achieve respectable accuracy and speed. It is a typical two-handed Weaver style grip with fingers on fingers and thumbs on thumbs, wrapped around the grip frame. The firing-side thumb rests along the left side of the weapon and the support-side thumb laps up next to it and lies somewhat over the firing side thumb. Both curl slightly forward toward the muzzle end of the weapon. The firing-side hand exerts forward pressure against the backstrap of the weapon and the support-side hand pulls back on the front strap to complete the isometric pressure feature of the grip. This pressure locks the weapon in the hands of the shooter and assists with recoil management when the weapon is being fired.

The pressure should be in the 50% to 50% range to start. The thumbs should exert no lateral pressure on the pistol, but they will, by virtue of their curled nature, assist with recoil management and limit the vertical rotation of the muzzle.

The IPSC/Thumbs Forward Grip

The grip system that is all the rage these days is the IPSC or Thumbs Forward Grip. It involves cradling the weapon in both hands with the thumbs distinctly pointing toward the target and resting along the left side of the gun. By virtue of its name, it is purely a competition grip system, designed by Brian Enos and Rob Leatham in the 1980s and used exclusively by the IPSC and IDPA competitors for many years. Law enforcement and the military have adopted it for certain units with good success.

Recently, Todd Jarrett and Para Ordnance have embarked on a marketing campaign to sell this grip to the general shooting public, *en masse*, as a one-

Several views of the Thumbs Forward Grip.

Several views of the Thumbs Forward Grip.

size-fits-all grip system. I personally feel that school is still out on this issue. The Thumbs Forward grip remains a competition-style grip designed by a competition shooter for competition shooters and is not well-suited for defensive handgun purposes. It is a complex system, very finicky and delicate and hard to master. It has varying pressure points on both axes (X and Y) that the shooter has to learn and engrain in order for the system to be effective for him.

Hours and hours of dry practice are necessary to fully master this grip. Add to that the fact that the isosceles stance normally accompanies the grip and one shoots with both eyes open, so good luck getting a hard focus on the front sight! Not the proper ingredients necessary for good defensive handgun techniques, in my opinion.

One good thing about the Thumbs Forward System is that the support-side index finger does not grip the front edge of the trigger guard. There is really no advantage to one's shooting accuracy by having the finger there, so this technique has fallen into much disfavor. We took extra efforts to discourage the gripping of the trigger guard in this manner at Front Sight. Very few instructors teach this technique anymore.

The AMW Grip

The third and final grip system is my Aggressive Modified Weaver or AMW, as I refer to it. At Front Sight we called it the Thumbs Stacked or Thumbs High grip.

The AMW Grip is a typical Weaver grip with an aggressive amount of forward and rearward hand pressure applied simultaneously to the frontstrap and backstrap of the gun. This pressure is termed isometric pressure and normally is 40% forward by the firing-side hand and 60% pull or rearward pressure by the support-side hand. The thumbs are stacked along the left side of the weapon and on a 1911A1 style pistol, the firing-side thumb resides on top of the thumb safety. The thumbs exert no lateral pressure on the left side of the pistol.

Note that the tips of the support-side hand are extended into space and make no contact with the back of the firing-side hand. This ensures that there is no lateral pressure from the right on the weapon. Having no lateral pressure from either side simplifies the grip and improves the chances for superior accuracy and shot delivery. The aggressive 40% to 60% front-to-rear pressure locks the weapon into the shooters hands and eliminates any need to re-grip the weapon after each shot. Vertical rotation of the muzzle is greatly diminished because of this grip pressure. Finally, front-to-rear pressure is the easiest to manage and control, unlike the pressures generated by more complicated grips that require hours and hours of dry practice just to learn the nuances and intricacies of pressure and hand position.

Finally, if a student has mastered the AMW grip and wishes to experiment with the IPSC grip system, he will find it much easier to understand and learn. He has built the perfect platform from which to master the complexities of the IPSC.

Performing the Aggressive Modified Weaver (AMW) Grip

For the purposes of this discussion, the explanation will be oriented to the right-handed shooter.

I teach my version of the modified Weaver grip and call it the Aggressive Modified Weaver (AMW). It is a single axis grip system, as opposed to most other grips that use some version of a dual axis system.

Your grip is the vise that holds the weapon steady for rapid, accurate shots without the need to constantly re-grip after every shot is fired. The AMW also is a superior grip when comes to recoil control and management.

To perform the AMW grip, place your firing-side hand high on the backstrap of the weapon with the web of your palm tight up against its tang. Now wrap the fingers of the firing-side hand firmly around the frontstrap of the grip frame.

In the case of shooting a Model 1911A-1, the firing-side thumb rests on top of the thumb safety while firing the weapon or doing any gun handling exercises. This is a requirement that must be observed faithfully to effectively operate this weapon. No pressure is exerted against the slide by the thumb. The support-side fingers are placed over the firing-side fingers, fingers on fingers, and wrapped around the grip frame. The support-side thumb is stacked next to the firing-side thumb high along side. No pressure is applied by the support-side thumb. Both thumbs are relaxed at this point. This grip setup is sometimes called Thumbs High, Thumb on Thumb or Thumbs Stacked.

Here is the "secret" part of this grip system. It requires the use of what is called isometric pressure, in which converging pressure is applied by the hands to the frontstrap and the backstrap simultaneously. It starts with the firing-side hand pushing forward toward the target against the backstrap while the support-side hand pulls back on the frontstrap away from the target. How much pressure? Enough to control the weapon under recoil and manage the vertical rotation of the barrel and muzzle. "Vertical rotation" – sometimes imprecisely referred to as "muzzle flip" or "recoil" – refers to the small imaginary vertical arc that the muzzle of the weapon traces in space each time the weapon is fired.

Note that there is no lateral or side pressure on the weapon. Very little or no contact with the stocks are made by the palms of the shooter. This is truly a single axis grip system. Front to back pressure helps stabilize any vertical movement of the muzzle.

How much fore-and-aft opposing pressure to apply will be determined by how much dry practice time you put into your stance and grip training. Start out at a 50-50 ratio of front to rear pressure. After you are comfortable with this percentage and feel you want to achieve further recoil control of your weapon, adjust the pressure to 60% to the rear and 40% forward. You will achieve greater mastery of the vertical rotation by doing it in this manner.

The firing-side arm can be locked out or slightly bent or flexed. It is a shooter's choice. The support-side elbow is bent and pointing straight down at the deck. The attitude of the elbow will add a lot of rearward pressure on the grip and assist in controlling the vertical rotation of the muzzle.

A Final Word

Grips can be categorized into several different usage applications. Based on their type of intended usage, there is a grip system for each purpose.

For instance, general recreational range shooting or plinking in the desert or woods, the shooter will be served best by the Thumb Over Thumb Weaver style grip. This grip is considered an excellent beginner's or entry-level system. I strongly recommend this grip to the new shooter and insist that they learn and master it. With some extensive professional instruction and experience on the range, they can go on to the AMW or other higher level grips.

In the self defense, personal protection scenario, the best grip is the AMW. It offers every feature that the concealed carry shooter is looking for. As stated above, the new shooter moving up in training and experience can adopt and learn the AMW when he is confident that he has the necessary training to master it quickly.

Competitive shooters have for years adopted and used the IPSC or Thumbs Forward Grip and it has served them well. Law enforcement and military units have used this system with excellent results. Other competitive events all have very specialized grip systems, all specific to that particular event. These systems do not lend themselves to general usage.

Hunting activity, in general, will need a diverse assortment of specialized grip systems, all based on caliber, type of game being hunted and distance to the target. Usually some variation of a Weaver grip is employed.

Because of the implications necessary for the self defense practitioner, the importance of a strong, aggressive grip is of the utmost importance. Multiple, deadly accurate shots may be fired. So, at the risk of repeating myself, the importance of a strong working grip is critical to self defense with a handgun, and the AMW Grip is the best overall choice for this application.

> *"One of the great delusions in the world is the hope that the evils of this world are to be cured by legislation."*
>
> Thomas B. Reed (1839-1902), Speaker of the House, 51st, 54th and 55th U.S. Congresses, 1886.

The firing side foot is placed four to six inches to the rear of the firing line and parallel to the support-side foot with both feet lined up parallel and facing at a 30° orientation to the target about shoulder length apart and facing to the right of the target for a right-handed shooter. Weight is on the balls of the feet and the knees are gently flexed.

Chapter 12

The Stance

The stance is a shooting platform that will facilitate a solid foundation from which the shooter can develop the ability to shoot with speed, precision and accuracy. I teach the Modified Weaver stance, which utilizes a 30° body blade as its prominent feature. Because it is the quintessential fighting stance, it affords the shooter great mobility to be able to move off quickly in any direction.

To assume this stance, the shooter first places the toe of his support-side foot on the firing line.

The firing side foot is now placed four to six inches to the rear of the firing line and parallel to the support-side foot. Both feet should now be lined up parallel and facing at a 30° orientation to the target. Both feet should be about shoulder length apart and facing to the right of the target, if you are a right-handed shooter. The direct opposite will be true for a left handed shooter. Weight should be on the balls of your feet and your knees gently flexed.

The shooter now bends slightly at the waist only. Shoulders, waist, knees and feet will all be bladed 30° from the target. Center of gravity should be just over the balls of the feet. The shooter turns the head toward the target and extends both arms in the same direction.

In the case of a right-handed shooter, as shown, the support-side hand will extend further to the target than the firing side hand.

Now bend slightly at the waist only. Your shoulders, waist, knees and feet will all be bladed 30° from the target. Your center of gravity should be just over the balls of your feet. Turn your head toward the target and extend both arms in the same direction. In the case of a right-handed shooter, the support-side hand will extend closer to the target than the firing side hand.

We have already covered the position and relationship of both arms.

> *"If you wish to become a really good shot you will learn to live with your gun."*
>
> Lt Col. Jeff Cooper.

Chapter 13

The Presentation

The presentation is often called the "draw" in many circles of our profession. I prefer the term "presentation": we present our weapons to a target, either real or on paper. We will also be presenting our weapons during our dry practice sessions.

Our presentation is a five-step procedure from the holster. It goes as follows;

Step #1: Face the target in a Weaver stance, eyes on target. Grip the grip frame of the weapon with your firing-side hand firmly and securely. Your support side palm now simultaneously moves to take a position in contact with your midsection.

Step 1. Face the target with hands at sides.

Step #2: Lift the weapon straight upward with your firing-side hand so that the muzzle just clears the top of the holster.

Step 2. Lift the weapon straight up and out of the holster.

Step #3: Move your firing-side elbow down and rotate it forward. The muzzle will rotate forward and to the horizontal and is now pointed downrange.

Step 3. Move your firing-side hand in a 90° arc so the weapon's muzzle points downrange.

Step #4: With your firing-side hand, move the weapon forward past your midsection as your support-side hand moves to acquire a two-handed grip on the weapon after the muzzle is clear of your body.

Step 4. Grasp the weapon with both hands.

Step #5: Continue to move your weapon downrange and upward until it is level with your line of sight.

Step 5. Continue moving the weapon downrange and up.

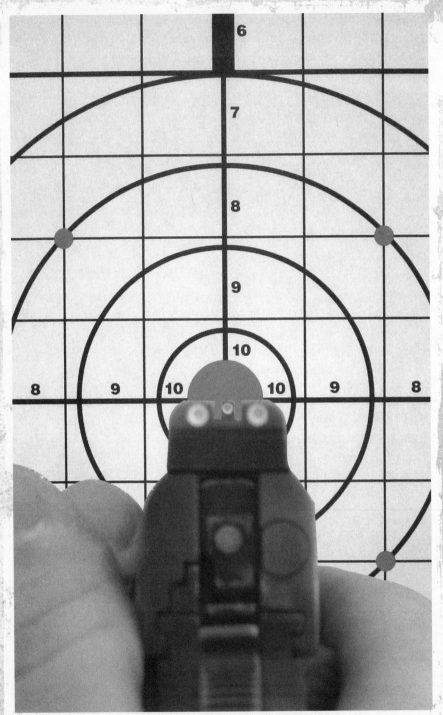

A perfectly-aligned sight picture. This shot will hit in the center of the bull.

Chapter 14

Sight Alignment, Sight Picture and Trigger Control (SST)

SST is my acronym for **S**ight Alignment, **S**ight Picture and **T**rigger Control. These techniques form the fundamental matrix for precision marksmanship skills. Without a total mastery of the SST principles, a shooter will never achieve the upper levels of marksmanship that would qualify him as a competitive or expert level shooter. Hours and hours of dry practice with these techniques is the only way to achieve this level of precision.

Sight Alignment

Sight alignment consists of properly aligning the front sight (and therefore the barrel) with your firing-side eye. Align the rectangular image of the front sight with the top of the ears of the rear sight. Both images should be straight and level across their tops. Equal slices of light should appear on both sides of the front image in the notch of the rear sight. This is perfect sight alignment.

Sight Picture

Sight picture is the act of taking this proper sight alignment and placing it on the target. It is the image of the front sight and the target that you see as you look through the rear sight notch. For defensive guncraft purposes, we place the proper sight alignment image on the very center of mass (COM) of any target at which we may be pointed in on.

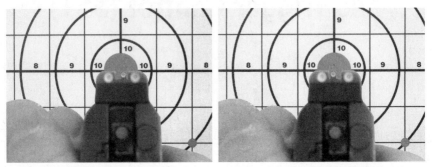

This shot will hit off-center, toward the right.   This shot will hit off-center, toward the left.

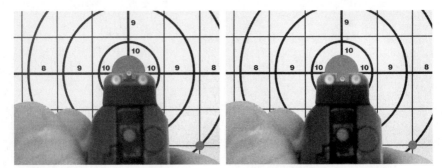

This shot will hit high.   This shot will hit low.

Trigger Control

This is the most important component of SST. It is also the hardest to accomplish and the easiest to lose. It consists of the relationship of the trigger finger and the controlled movement of the trigger to the rear. In the next chapter, which deals specifically with Trigger Control, under the Single Action Semi-automatic section, there is a detailed description of the proper technique to employ when operating the trigger of 1911A1-type firearm.

One of the key considerations to undertake is that you must NEVER allow your trigger finger to lose contact with the trigger at any time during the firing of your firearm.

Chapter 15

Trigger Control

The foundation of all world-class marksmanship is Trigger Control. When combined with proper sight alignment and proper sight picture, it forms the critical combination of factors that allow the shooter to achieve whatever level of precision he desires.

Trigger Control is a very difficult technique to understand, achieve and hold on to. It is a very perishable commodity that evaporates rapidly in the stress of competition or a gunfight or through lack of dry practice. Hours of dry practice are necessary to hone and master your Trigger Control skills and raise them to the level of precision desired.

Because there are two basic types of trigger actions (single action and double action), there are two finger placement settings. Remember that single action refers to handguns in which the hammer is cocked either by the action of the slide or by the shooter's thumb; double action refers to handguns in which the trigger cocks either a visible hammer or, on some models of pistol, a concealed striker.

Single Action Trigger: Semiautomatic Pistol

Start with a cocked gun, safety off. Place the trigger finger on the trigger face with the tip of the finger pad just resting over the bow of the trigger. If properly done, the finger should achieve a 90° bend from the second knuckle to the body of the hand.

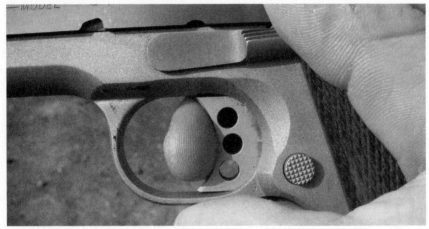

Place pad of trigger finger on trigger.

Placing the trigger finger on the trigger, start a gentle press to the rear to take the slack out of the trigger mechanism. You will notice that a pressure resistance will suddenly build in the trigger. This is called mechanical resistance or "trigger stacking." Focus on the front sight is very important here. Pause, then start slow, steady pressure to the rear, which will result in the shot finally breaking. Hold the trigger to the rear for a moment.

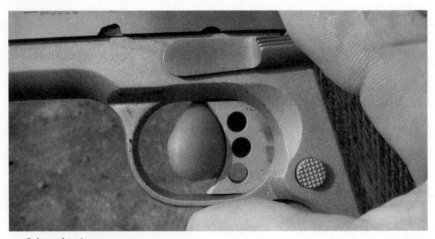

Release the trigger to reset.

Now release the trigger to go forward so that it resets. Trigger reset can be identified by an audible click or a slight "bump" in the trigger mechanism against your trigger finger.

With the trigger finger still on the trigger, pause a moment and restart the press to the rear. This will result in the firing of a second shot or additional shots, if the process is repeated.

Double Action Trigger: Semiautomatic Pistol or Revolver

Place the trigger finger on the trigger at approximately the center of the first joint.

Place finger on trigger at center of first joint.

Because of the trigger pressure and length of travel of the trigger, sufficient leverage is needed to draw the trigger fully to the rear. Pressure to the rear should be slow, steady and continuous.

Press trigger, using slow, continuous pressure.

Do not stage the trigger – i.e., do not jerk it or squeeze in a series of movements – and let the shot break. Let the trigger go forward and start the press over again. Your trigger finger should stay in contact with the trigger face at all times.

Double/single Action Trigger: Semiautomatic Pistol

Double/single action pistols are those in which the first shot is fired through a long double-action trigger squeeze and subsequent shots are fired single action.

Because in this type of pistol we have two trigger actions to deal with, the shooter has a couple of options to consider when firing his weapon. The first round is fired double action. All subsequent rounds are fired single action. Normally, as discussed above, single action and double action triggers each require a different trigger technique.

Modern day guncraft instruction advocates placing the pad of the trigger finger on the trigger and pressing the trigger to the rear for double/single action pistols, not changing the position of the trigger finger to accommodate the separate trigger actions. The first round is therefore the most difficult to hold on the target due to the building of the trigger pressure and the time required to achieve shot break.

Lately, however, conventional wisdom recommends firing the double/single action trigger with the trigger finger placed at the first distal joint and leaving it in that position for all subsequent shots fired in the single action mode. It was formerly held that this technique risks pulling the muzzle off the target due to the tendency to pull across the trigger with the reduced angle of the finger on the trigger. However, I recently tested a SIG Model 225 at a local range in this manner and found no reduction in my accuracy. In fact, I continued to get center-of-mass hits with no problems or loss of speed of delivery. I now teach this method of firing a D/S action pistol to all my students.

> *"The pistol is a poor assault weapon. It is an instrument for stopping a gun fight before it begins."*
>
> Lt Col. Jeff Cooper.

Chapter 16

Reloading Drills

Reloads are procedures by which a shooter is able to replentish the weapon with ammunition either during a gun fight or during a lull in that fight. The need for reloading can be either immediate or a matter of choice, depending on the circumstances.

There are three types of reloads: Emergency, Tactical, and Administrative.

Emergency Reload

In an emergency reload, you have fired the weapon empty to slide lock and must now reload.

Upon realizing that the weapon is empty, reach for a fresh magazine in your magazine pouch. Punch out the empty magazine as you move the open end of the magazine to the magazine well.

Reach for a full magazine.

Punch out the empty magazine.

Briskly and firmly insert the magazine into the magazine well. Release the slide stop, or pull back slightly on the slide and release it, to recharge the weapon; point in assess; and fire, if necessary.

Rack the slide, point in, assess and fire.

Tactical Reload

The tactical reload is reloading the weapon when you want to top off the firearm before you have fired it empty. It is normally done during a lull in the gunfight when there is no danger of putting yourself at risk of being shot. To perform a tactical reload:

Bring the gun to your midsection while securing a fresh magazine from the magazine pouch with your support-side hand.

Retrieve a fully-loaded magazine from the pouch.

Bring the fully-loaded magazine to the magazine well.

Bring the magazine close to the magazine well.

Drop the partially-full magazine in the magazine well into your upturned palm and insert the fresh magazine briskly into the magazine well.

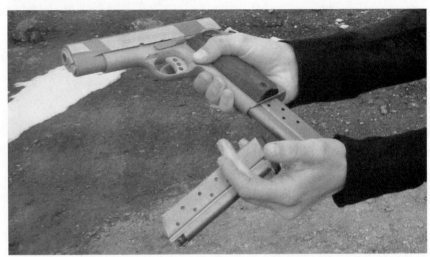

Eject the partially-full magazine into your palm and insert the fully-loaded magazine.

Firmly seat the fresh magazine.

Firmly seat the fresh magazine. Stow the ejected magazine in your pouch or pocket. (There is no need to fully rack the slide since there is already a round in the chamber.)

Administrative Reload

This is the simple loading procedure, as we discussed earlier in the Loading and Unloading chapter. It is normally performed at the start of a firing exercise.

Chapter 17

Malfunction Clearances

A malfunction is a stoppage during the cycling of a weapon that is normally the result of operator error or faulty ammunition. It can be cleared and the weapon put back in action in a matter of seconds.

A malfunction is often incorrectly called a "jam" by many students and pundits in the media. Simply put, a jam is nothing more than the mechanical breakage or failure of an internal part or parts that causes the weapon to stop cycling. Normally, tools or a gunsmith are needed to get the firearm back into action. This will require a considerable amount of time to fix – something there is never enough of in a gunfight!

There are three types of malfunctions that you must master:

- **Type #1.** Failure to Fire
- **Type #2.** Failure to Eject (Stove Pipe Malfunction)
- **Type #3** Failure to Extract Feedway Stoppage
  ("The Mother of all Malfunctions")

Type #1 Clearance: Tap, Rack, Flip, Point In

Tap the magazine well area firmly to be sure the magazine is seated.

Rack the slide to the rear to remove a faulty or stuck round and chamber a fresh round.

Point in, assess and fire, if necessary.

Type #2 Clearance: Look, Tap, Rack, Flip, Point In

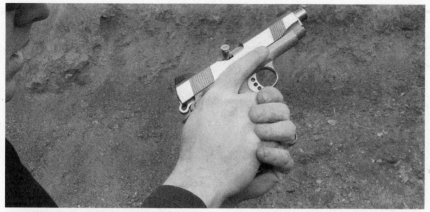

Tip the weapon muzzle slightly upward and observe ejection port area.

Tap the magazine well area firmly to seat the magazine.

Flip the weapon to the right while racking the slide to free the casing.

Type #2 continued

Flip the weapon to the right while racking the slide to free the casing.

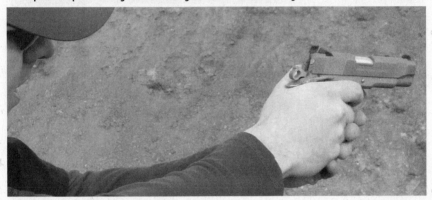

Point in to reacquire the target, assess and fire, if necessary.

Type #3. Clearance: Look, Lock, Strip, Rack, Rack, Rack, Insert, Rack, Point In

Tip the muzzle of the weapon slightly up and look into the ejection port to identify the problem.

Type #3. continued

Lock the slide to the rear.

Press magazine release and strip the magazine from gun.

Rapidly rack the slide three times to remove any stuck rounds.

Type #3. continued

Insert a fresh magazine.

Rack the slide to arm the weapon and point in. Point in to reacquire the target, assess and fire, if necessary.

Chapter 18

After Action Drills

After Action Drills are range exercises that condition you and duplicate what may happen out on the street following a gun fight between you and a violent adversary. This procedure attempts to simulate the action you would take immediately following an exchange of gunfire. Remember, this drill does not establish a cast-in-concrete set of rules for the student to follow. What you would actually do, in any case, will depend on the actual conditions that are present at that time.

The drill consists of three separate stages that are undertaken in succession one after the other.

Stage #1: Quick Check

The quick check consists of rapid side to side movement of the head to look to the right and the left of your position. You are looking to see if a bad guy has moved in very near to you.

The quick check.

Stage #2: Final Check

The final check is a deliberate look downrange to find your adversary, assess his condition and determine whether he still poses a threat to you.

The final check.

Stage #3: Scan

This is a slow, deliberate 360° scan of the complete area surrounding your position. You are searching for any additional accomplices of the adversary that may want to get involved in this fight.

The scan.

Cover and Concealment

Based on what your scan tells you about your attacker, you may choose to engage him from cover or conceal yourself. The difference between the two is that cover protects you from being hit by an incoming round while concealment simply hides you from the attacker's view.

Cover.

Concealment.

Chapter 19

The Future of Defensive Handgun Skills

So where is all this going? Certainly firearms ownership, CCW permits and armed citizens carrying in public is not for everyone, but gun ownership and more citizens legally carrying weapons, coupled with the proliferation of private gun schools, has decreased violent crime in the United States.

We know that gun ownership is rising at an ever-increasing rate compared to a decade ago. The National Shooting Sports Federation (NSSF) states that, as of this writing, there are now nearly 65 million gun owners in the U.S. When you contrast that with the gun control/confiscation folly happening in the U.K, Australia and Canada and the steady increase in the number of gun-related crimes committed in those countries, it should make you pause and think this issue over from a non-biased perspective.

All three of these nations have reported and will no doubt continue to report a noticeable rise in the occurrence of violent gun-related crimes. Their response to this phenomenon is to enact more draconian gun control laws. Go figure. Part of their problem is that they refuse to accept the premise that the mere presence of lawfully- and responsibly-owned firearms in any given locale does not represent any particular danger to anyone and actually reduces violent crime.

Another major ingredient in this equation is the increased availability of professional firearms training institutes. Many more gun schools have been established in the last two decades. The true reason for the drop in crime is attributable to and concurrent with the rise in the number of law-abiding, trained, legally permitted armed citizens on the streets of the United States. As stated earlier, the criminal element is not anxious to meet an armed citizen. I have said often and loudly to all who would listen or are within earshot, these cowards have no interest in being confronted by an armed citizen with a firearm.

NICS Firearm Background Checks
Year 2009
January 1, 2009 - November 30, 2009

STATE	JAN	FEB	MAR	APR	MAY	JUN	JUL	AUG	SEP	OCT	NOV	DEC	TOTALS
Alabama	29,770	30,391	27,949	21,322	20,277	18,538	21,001	24,123	24,221	27,346	30,734		275,672
Alaska	4,227	4,652	5,140	5,775	4,878	4,419	4,263	5,076	4,885	6,724	4,726		54,765
Arizona	20,293	21,423	21,766	20,896	17,837	18,953	16,099	14,956	14,619	14,831	14,003		195,676
Arkansas	17,819	21,434	19,172	19,326	13,435	14,489	14,074	14,319	15,465	18,480	18,795		186,808
California	72,039	62,736	72,248	73,315	64,304	63,190	61,389	65,927	62,920	64,468	56,392		718,928
Colorado	28,193	29,189	32,067	30,277	27,595	24,127	20,949	22,782	21,855	22,940	24,466		284,440
Connecticut	18,593	19,264	21,879	19,564	16,972	16,887	15,338	15,081	15,448	14,754	13,520		187,300
Delaware	1,860	1,886	2,031	1,736	1,439	1,318	1,245	1,545	1,520	1,763	1,926		18,269
District of Columbia	34	40	40	34	29	28	25	31	28	28	33		350
Florida	51,169	53,862	55,646	48,761	40,976	38,505	38,918	40,232	39,874	44,824	46,324		499,091
Georgia	39,703	44,226	40,635	30,714	24,765	24,872	23,360	25,045	24,701	28,353	27,511		333,885
Guam	54	34	27	40	38	45	34	42	41	50	43		448
Hawaii	894	792	1,086	1,013	897	758	813	687	867	853	859		9,519
Idaho	8,903	9,851	11,281	9,396	6,886	6,798	6,207	6,930	7,615	8,237	7,406		89,510
Illinois	62,068	58,938	72,066	82,671	64,049	52,126	47,204	54,912	60,010	65,610	64,018		683,672
Indiana	23,196	24,131	25,741	20,245	16,093	14,038	14,138	19,136	25,710	29,405	29,522		241,355
Iowa	11,987	11,199	13,542	10,764	7,354	6,646	6,309	7,213	8,711	11,807	11,146		106,478
Kansas	14,131	13,268	14,201	11,607	9,031	7,979	8,181	10,762	10,137	13,343	14,017		126,657
Kentucky	167,035	173,104	175,314	174,987	174,703	175,957	179,312	182,433	187,031	194,580	195,656		1,980,112
Louisiana	22,219	21,839	21,087	17,171	14,561	13,579	15,059	18,088	25,613	22,882	22,585		214,443
Maine	4,200	4,676	5,782	5,148	3,948	3,763	3,847	4,406	5,887	7,967	5,444		55,068
Mariana Islands	0	0	0	0	0	0	0	0	0	0	0		0
Maryland	8,734	9,271	9,733	8,445	6,328	6,453	6,344	6,379	7,152	8,169	9,498		86,506
Massachusetts	8,960	8,230	10,135	9,236	7,827	7,487	6,730	6,682	7,681	8,887	8,631		90,486
Michigan	30,182	32,473	38,803	34,713	25,954	24,233	23,268	26,423	28,759	31,974	32,954		329,736
Minnesota	22,768	23,895	32,695	31,130	19,636	18,162	17,426	21,487	25,748	29,398	20,902		263,247
Mississippi	16,201	16,599	13,189	11,131	9,488	8,359	9,717	11,702	12,488	14,967	18,202		142,043
Missouri	32,110	35,664	36,214	30,743	23,401	21,868	21,998	26,207	26,143	33,121	30,743		318,212
Montana	7,519	8,799	9,600	9,076	8,190	7,541	7,082	8,311	8,753	10,521	7,326		92,718
Nebraska	5,702	5,475	6,092	5,495	3,211	3,379	3,103	4,108	4,638	6,017	5,792		53,012
Nevada	10,224	10,154	11,536	10,912	8,004	7,695	6,908	7,597	6,985	8,224	8,367		96,606
New Hampshire	6,165	5,910	7,376	6,975	5,463	4,896	5,239	6,019	6,327	8,681	6,536		69,587
New Jersey	4,216	4,343	5,266	5,060	4,587	4,739	4,428	4,172	4,083	4,953	4,713		50,540
New Mexico	9,635	10,875	10,757	8,676	7,901	7,762	7,168	8,333	8,047	8,776	7,963		95,893
New York	18,383	18,910	22,794	21,727	16,415	16,193	15,824	17,289	21,159	25,423	23,176		217,293
North Carolina	38,538	39,872	37,632	31,413	25,730	23,591	22,884	24,625	25,737	29,399	30,279		329,700
North Dakota	3,523	3,682	3,648	4,714	4,078	3,289	3,439	4,419	5,749	4,107			43,779
Ohio	33,593	38,939	41,762	35,416	27,137	24,817	25,287	26,574	27,796	33,727	39,266		354,314
Oklahoma	22,098	24,547	21,680	21,163	16,353	13,868	14,753	17,083	16,049	18,934	21,832		208,359
Oregon	16,799	18,063	20,906	16,980	14,086	12,127	11,007	12,204	14,503	14,610	14,938		166,223
Pennsylvania	54,695	57,544	69,675	59,806	45,804	43,428	42,862	44,917	50,424	56,079	60,101		585,335
Puerto Rico	625	609	727	653	637	663	658	689	715	705	585		7,266
Rhode Island	1,287	1,355	1,557	1,469	1,158	1,072	922	968	1,098	1,355	1,186		13,427
South Carolina	17,818	20,958	19,681	18,209	15,961	13,977	14,914	15,567	16,028	16,984	21,990		192,087
South Dakota	5,447	5,614	5,776	5,533	3,769	3,786	3,652	4,757	5,738	7,578	5,742		57,392
Tennessee	31,505	33,801	34,899	26,003	25,506	23,435	26,032	55,766	27,528	35,780	40,591		360,846
Texas	86,835	96,192	102,372	76,844	71,891	69,421	66,285	80,589	74,929	78,429	95,339		899,126
Utah	28,809	16,137	18,402	28,052	16,119	19,092	31,518	20,191	15,749	30,908	12,993		237,970
Vermont	1,619	2,314	2,456	2,129	1,564	1,349	1,437	1,644	2,028	2,421	2,068		21,029
Virgin Islands	183	126	179	213	162	169	120	136	147	113	117		1,665
Virginia	27,133	29,763	28,923	26,103	19,811	17,106	20,436	20,882	21,425	27,563	27,434		266,579
Washington	31,526	33,303	35,861	32,498	27,031	23,229	21,284	23,384	24,405	27,301	24,453		304,275
West Virginia	13,020	15,097	13,698	12,237	10,016	9,232	9,628	10,435	12,343	15,987	17,419		139,112
Wisconsin	14,071	17,025	23,883	19,575	11,864	10,519	10,498	14,794	17,700	21,119	19,327		180,346
Wyoming	4,553	5,050	5,594	4,931	4,202	4,118	3,421	3,800	3,804	3,663	3,553		46,689

NOTE: The totals above indicate the number of firearm background checks requested. The totals do not indicate firearm transfers.

As evidenced by the growing number of federal background checks, lawful firearms ownership in the United States is on the rise.

It is my considered opinion that the concept of the armed citizen as a crime deterrent is growing in acceptance by the American public and, surprisingly, by many local governments as well. The gun-owning public is saying, in effect, that we will step up and accept the responsibility for our own safety and protection. It is an awesome and demanding responsibility, but one that will reap enormous and long-term satisfaction and peace of mind for all.

Chapter 20

Interesting and Useful Odds and Ends

I have always wondered where I was going to put all the witticisms, sayings and related pearls of wisdom that abound in our field of firearms and firearms training. These are the thoughts and words that just don't fit anywhere else or do not lend themselves to the length of a full chapter. I suppose this is as good a place as any.

Tactical Training and Dry Practice

In order to establish a training regimen for dry practice, live fire and perhaps even concealed carry, you will need to research and decide the type of firearm you will train with and ultimately carry.

Pick only one weapon to train with. It will ultimately become your carry weapon, should you decide that your journey will end there. It can be either a pistol (autoloader) or a revolver.

Here are the variables you must consider when choosing a weapon. A few of them are widely agreed on (for example, .the .380 ACP or .38 Special cartridge is generally considere to be the smallest that can be relied on for self defense), while others are purely a matter of personal preference.

- Bullet caliber
- Size of the weapon
- Model of the weapon
- Weight of the weapon
- Firepower (capacity)
- Barrel length
- Action (double or single)
- Anatomy (hand size and the shooter's strength)
- Stock size (configuration of stock to hand size)

Dry Practice

Live fire will serve to validate your progress with your dry practice training. It is not intended to provide the student with any form of fun or entertainment.

Your goal for your marksmanship drills is to develop the ability to deliver two sighted shots to the thoracic cavity of your target at 7 meters in 1.5 seconds with about 95% consistency. Ideally, these shots should print about two inches apart. This should ensure your survival in a gun fight.

The head shot will virtually guarantee your survival. It is a precision, sighted shot and needs to require about two to three seconds to achieve.

Tactical Training

There are three types of shooting disciplines:

Recreational Shooting

• Helps the student understands the basic fundamentals of firearms nomenclature and simple marksmanship.

Bullseye and Competition Shooting

Includes all of the above benefits and adds the discipline of execution. It further adds stress via time constraints around slow and rapid fire at a fixed target. Bullseye shooters must present their weapons from the holster rapidly, solve complex range problems and get quality hits with precision. Long distance bullseye competition is not a consideration here.

Tactical Shooting

Its demands include all of the above, but it includes the principles of tactics (movement) and the psychology of a combat mindset combined with an emphasis on survival. Time constraints can also be added, if desired.

Gun Fighting

Gun fighting, as most of us know it, is what we see in the movies or on the television. We can all put some stock in the knowledge that most of it is the figment of some Hollywood writer's imagination. However, in our heart of hearts, we know that from historical evidence, a certain percentage of that sort of sudden violence did happen.

So, indulging our fantasies, gun fighting requires a combination of precision (accuracy) and speed to insure survival. Of the two ingredients, precision is the most important.

Some random quotations that have survived the test of time are included below. The authors of these quotations are not known, but I will still put quotes around them, in deference to those responsible for their creation.

> *"You can be an excellent pistol shot and not be a good gunfighter."*

> *"If you are an excellent gunfighter, you are probably an excellent shooter [marksman]."*

> *"There is no such thing as an advanced gunfight. Just gunfights in which the fundamentals are executed at differing levels."*

I have reason to suspect that the latter quotation can be attributed to none other than Col. Jeff Cooper.

There is no way to totally prepare for that dreaded gun fight unless you adhere to a regular dry practice routine. That will help, because the variables you will face are myriad. As is true for any athlete, training is the answer to increase your survival chances. Practicing all the combat scenarios you can imagine is the secret here. Practice them all until they become totally reflexive in nature. You need to be on autopilot while doing them.

Here are some of the conditions you will encounter in a typical gun fight environment:

- Chaos
- Noise
- Close Distances
- Confusion
- Fear, stress and anxiety
- Very short duration (5-10 seconds to a couple of minutes)
- Movement seemingly in slow motion, referred to as tachypsychia
- Tunnel vision

Your responses here should be:

- Move and shoot.
- Shoot and move.
- Shoot while moving.
- Seek cover and/or concealment, then shoot.

Standing out in the open and engaging your adversary is not a good option, unless you know that you have the advantage (drop) on him. Your training and dry practice regimen and survival instincts should take over to ensure your reaction to the threat and your survival of it.

After reading Frank James's excellent book, *Effective Handgun Defense*, I feel compelled to share a portion of Chapter Two, page 28 with you. His book is a well-researched, technical and informative examination of concealed carry and defensive handgun techniques.

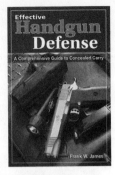

A must-read:
Effective Handgun Defense
by Frank James.

With Frank's permission, I will quote verbatim from the section on the Rules of Gun Fighting. I know that many of you may be familiar with some of these rules, most of which are tongue-in-cheek and some of which are serious efforts at explaining a gunfight and gun handling. They have an honest and creditable sense about them.

Frank credits several writers and gun authorities with the creation of these rules and I will only suggest that their names can be found in the aforementioned book.

Enjoy.

The Rules Of Gun Fighting
They are as follows:

Have a Gun. This is the absolute First Rule of Gun Fighting and can be properly attributed to Mark Moritz, an attorney living in Arizona.

If at all possible, have at least two guns and even better, make sure one of them is a long gun, preferably a rifle with a high-capacity magazine.

Bring all of your friends who have guns. (The United States Marine Corps performs this theory and remains among its better practitioners.)

Anything worth shooting is worth shooting twice. Ammo is cheap. Life is valuable. When the prosecutor asks, "Why did you shoot this deceased twice?" The answer is, "because I was trained to do so!"

Only hits count. A miss with the most powerful gun you own is still a miss. Shoot and carry what you can hit with. (That is incorrect grammar, but it is perfect logic.)

Proximity negates skill. Distance is your friend. You can't go to the store and buy time, but you can create distance between you and your adversary through lateral or diagonal movement and achieve the same result as buying time. If you can create a distance greater than 21 feet between you and your adversary, the mathematical odds for survival weigh heavily in your favor.

Accuracy is relative. RELIABILITY IS NOT. You must use a gun that works all the time – Every Time. If it doesn't work, get a different gun or better ammo or both. No excuses.

If your shooting stance is good, you're probably not moving fast enough or using cover properly.

Always cheat. Always win. The only unfair fight is the one you lose.

If you are not shooting, you should be communicating, reloading your weapon and moving.

Someday someone will kill you with your own gun, but they should have to beat you to death with it because it is empty.

Always have a plan.

Always have a backup plan, because in all probability the first plan won't work.

Use cover and concealment as much as possible.

Flank your adversary whenever possible, but protect your own flanks.

Decide to be aggressive enough, quickly enough.

Watch their hands. Hands kill. However, once the weapon appears, this issue has been decided. Now move to the next issue and watch their eyes because their eyes may telegraph their future movement.

The faster you finish the fight, the less chance you will have of getting shot.

Always perform a tactical reload whenever possible and scan for threats left, right and to the rear.

Carry the same gun in the same place all the time.

Your number one option for personal security is a lifelong commitment to Avoidance, Deterrence and De-Escalation.

Be polite. Be professional. Be courteous to everyone. Trust no one.

In 10 years nobody will remember the details of caliber, stance or tactics. They will only remember who lived.

"Do unto others as they would do unto you, only do it first!"

Western frontier adage. No known source.

Glossary

ACTION: The moving parts contained within the frame of a firearm that allow it to cycle and be fired.

AFTER ACTION DRILL: Movements executed by the shooter after he has fired his weapon during a gun fight that will provide for improved safety and protection against the possibility of any additional lethal attacks.

AUTOLOADER: A pistol that is capable of reloading itself with the cycling of the slide. Also called a SEMIAUTOMATIC PISTOL or simply SEMIAUTO.

CONCEALMENT: A barrier that will hide the shooter from view but not necessarily from any shots fired into that barrier.

BACKSTRAP: The rear vertical portion of the frame of a pistol or revolver that lies between the stock panels.

BARREL: The rifled metal tube through which the bullet travels when the shot breaks.

BORE: The open inside portion of the barrel.

BREAK THE SHOT: The act of firing the weapon.

CARTRIDGE: A complete, unfired round. It contains the case, primer, powder and bullet (projectile).

CENTERFIRE: A cartridge with the primer centered in the base of the case.

CHAMBER: The open rear of the barrel into which the cartridge is placed prior to being fired.

CHAMBER CHECK: The act of easing the slide back approximately ¼" to expose the presence of a cartridge, thus determining that the weapon is either empty or loaded.

CONTROLLED PAIR: Two sighted shots fired at the intended target, each with a distinct, conscious sight picture.

COVER: A barrier that will protect you from any shots fired at you.

CROSS-EYED DOMINANT: The condition that occurs when your dominant firing side eye and your firing-side hand are opposite from one another. Example; Dominant eye is your right eye, firing-side hand is your left hand.

CYCLE OF OPERATION: The total function of a pistol from shot break, ejection of empty cartridge, stripping and loading of new full cartridge into the chamber and locking of slide into battery. For a revolver, it involves breaking the shot, rotation of the cylinder and alignment of barrel and the next chamber.

CYLINDER: The elongated, round metal part in the centerline of the revolver frame that holds cartridges in the individual chambers. On a double action revolver, the cylinder advances a round one chamber at a time with each press of the trigger.

DECOCKING LEVER: The lever on many semiautomatics that allows the shooter to safely lower the hammer down on the firing pin from the cocked position.

DOUBLE ACTION: The action of a firearm where the trigger mechanism can both cock the hammer and then release the hammer to strike the firing pin by simply pressing the trigger all the way to the rear.

DOUBLE TAP: The act of firing two quick shots at your intended target with only one sight picture.

DRY PRACTICE: The act of practicing gun handling and marksmanship techniques without any ammunition in the weapon.

EMERGENCY RELOAD: An operational technique to reload a fresh magazine into the weapon after it has been fired empty to slide lock.

EJECTOR: A frame mounted metal part that the spent cartridge case strikes on its travel to the rear. The case is then ejected out the ejection port opening in the slide.

FAILURE TO STOP DRILL: A self protection two-step shooting procedure where by the shooter fires two sighted shots into the thoracic cavity of his attacker, comes down to the ready position, pauses, realizes that his attacker is still a threat, comes up to the point in position and fires an aimed, precision shot to his head to end the fight.

FIRING PIN: The slender spring-loaded metal part in the slide/bolt face that contacts the primer on the rear of the cartridge when the hammer is released. In the revolver, the firing pin is usually located, under spring tension, at the upper rear back strap portion of the frame

FIRING SIDE: The side of the shooter's body from which the weapon is fired.

FLASH SIGHT PICTURE: A quick but not fully aligned sight picture that allows the shooter to quickly fire his weapon. This method of shooting is normally used at very short distances where speed of the shot is most important and accuracy is secondary.

FRAME: The main body of a firearm that contains a majority of the moving parts of the weapon.

FRONT STRAP: The front vertical edge of the frame of a pistol located below the trigger guard.

GRIP: The main part of the frame by which a shooter holds the firearm, here it is used as a noun, in the verb form, it is what the shooter does to shoot his weapon.

GRIP FRAME: That portion of the firearm's frame that the shooter grabs in order to hold or fire the weapon.

HAMMER: The metal part under spring tension that, when released by the sear, drops and strikes the firing pin to fire the weapon. It is normally located in the upper backstrap of the gun and can be external (visible) or internal (hidden).

HANG FIRE: A perceptible delay in cartridge ignition after the hammer has dropped on the firing pin.

JAM: A failure or breakage of internal parts of the weapon that causes a stoppage in operation.

MAGAZINE: The elongated, boxlike metal storage device that holds the cartridges in a semiauto pistol. It is inserted into the magazine well at the base of the grip frame.

MAGAZINE RELEASE: A metal button device usually located on the grip frame of a semiautomatic pistol behind the trigger guard which, when depressed, locks the magazine into or releases it from the magazine well. Certain European models have the release button located on the heal of the grip frame butt, just behind the magazine well.

MAGAZINE WELL: The hollow portion of the grip frame that holds the loaded magazine.

MALFUNCTION: An operational failure of a weapon usually caused by operator error or faulty ammunition.

MUZZLE: The open end of the barrel of the weapon out of which the bullet exits the firearm.

PIE OFF: (pie a corner) A movement technique of incrementally sidestepping around a corner to safely clear the other side of that area.

PRESENTATION: The moving of the weapon from the holster to the point in position. Also called the DRAW.

+P: A classification of ammunition that is loaded to a higher pressure than standard factory loads.

+P+: A classification of ammunition that is loaded to a higher pressure than +P ammunition.

READY POSITION: An alert position in which the shooter positions his weapon at a 45 degree angle to the horizontal.

RIMFIRE: A cartridge that has its primer material deposited on the inside of the case around the base, in a small, circular lip that extends outward beyond the sidewall of the case. The most popular rimfire cartridge is the .22 Long Rifle.

SEMIAUTOMATIC: Refers to the definition of a self-loading firearm.

SIGHTS: The iron, optical or electronic sighting devices mounted of the top strap or slide of a firearm.

SINGLE ACTION: The action of a pistol in which the trigger only releases the hammer to fire the weapon. To allow the weapon to fire, the hammer must first be manually cocked.

SLIDE ACTION RELEASE: On a semiauto pistol, the lever that locks the slide open or releases it.

SLIDE: The large metal upper portion of most semiauto pistols that travels alternately to the back and front on the top of the frame as a shot is fired.

SUPPORT SIDE: The side of the body that assists in the firing of the weapon.

TACHYPSYCHIA: The sensation created by extreme stress, anxiety and fear that everything about a person is moving in slow motion.

TACTICAL RELOAD: The act of exchanging a partially full magazine with a fully loaded magazine. Done during a lull in a gunfight to increase the firepower of the weapon.

TRIGGER: The component that fires a weapon when the shooter depresses it with a finger.

TRIGGER GUARD: The metal ring portion of the weapon that surrounds and protects the trigger.

TYPE I MALFUNCTION: A failure to fire.

TYPE II MALFUNCTION: A failure to eject.

TYPE III MALFUNCTION: A failure to feed.

VERTICAL ROTATION: This a modern term for the older term "muzzle flip" to describe the movement of the muzzle up and back under cartridge ignition and subsequent recoil.

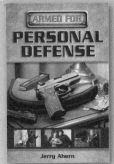
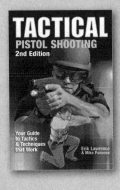
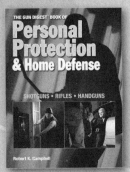
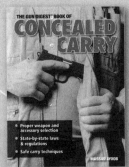